Death by Leadership

Dr. Joseph H. Fleishman

Dedication

To my wife, Susan C. Fleishman, who remains a constant inspiration to me.

Mr. William Scriber - High School English Teacher. Mr. Scriber was an amazing man whose influence continues to shape my life.

To paraphrase Sir Winston Churchill in summarizing our nation's current leadership conundrum,
"Never before have so few…done so little…for so many."

"You can't beat out of the flesh what was born in the marrow of the bone."
Anonymous

Hubris only knows ignorance.

This book provides accurate and authoritative information in regard to the theory of Forensic Leadership Pathology. The information is given with the understanding that the author is not engaged in rendering legal, professional advice. Since the details of your situation are fact dependent, you should seek additional services of a competent professional.

All Case Studies are written for instructional purposes only. All individuals are presumed innocent until proven guilty in a court of law.

Published in the United States of America
Business & Economics / Leadership
Management / Teamwork
Covalent Leadership

16.11.25

Thank you for your support of Fleishmanbooks.com.

Table of Contents

Introduction

"Be with a leader when he is right, stay with him when he is still right, but, leave when he is wrong."
Abraham Lincoln

Forensics Leadership Analysis

Leadership in America today is horribly broken. It is broken because leaders in the public and private sectors are encouraged, and often handsomely rewarded, for introducing a wide variety of malignant leadership behaviors which, over time, disrupt and destroy an organization from the top down.

The purpose of this book, Death by Leadership, is not to fix all the dysfunctional leaders in the world because there are simply too many of them. Rather, this book provides the millions of individuals working for organizations whose leadership is woefully under prepared for the responsibility of leading others, with the skills and knowledge to discern which leaders are worth following and which leaders should be avoided like the plague they are.

For the past thirty years, I have had the opportunity to work with a variety of leaders in the public and private sectors from across the country. If my experience has taught me anything, it is this, the lesson taught to me by my grandfather nearly forty years ago is as true today as it was when he first shared it with me at the time, "Joseph," he said, "you can't fix stupid!" My Grandfather, Herston Cromer, was a very wise man.

Now, forty years and thousands of leaders later, I have come to appreciate and understand the reason you can't fix stupid—stupid simply refuses to be fixed.

The predicament facing millions of incumbent and first-time individuals entering the workforce today is how to avoid working for an organization whose leadership is not worth following. While most well-adjusted, talented, capable, and competent individuals do not *want* to work for a boss from hell, many individuals, through no fault of their own, find themselves stuck in this exact predicament. Why? The answer is most people are not able to recognize and identify the malignant behaviors introduced by dysfunctional leaders for what they are when they see and experience them first-hand.

Death by Leadership borrows heavily from the field of forensic medicine to provide the reader with the skills, knowledge, and tools to perform a real-time Leadership Autopsy. Just as a medical autopsy provides a clear, scientific understanding concerning the primary cause of death of an individual, a Leadership Autopsy allows us to see and understand the full impact a dysfunctional leader has on an organization, in real-time.

Death by Leadership provides individuals with the tools, skills, and knowledge necessary to determine for themselves if they are working for an organization whose leadership is worth following or nothing more than a Lead Conductor on a train headed straight to Dysfunctionville.

Welcome to the exciting field of Forensics Leadership Pathology.

Function of Leadership

"There has never been such an army before.
These men will go anywhere and do anything if they are properly led."
Confederate General Robert E. Lee

In his role as the Commander of the Army of Northern Virginia, General Robert E. Lee succinctly summed up the essence of leadership; *to lead properly*. The primary function of a leader is to inspire others to excel in ways they never dreamed possible. Lee stated clearly to Confederate President Jefferson Davis from the very beginning that he saw his role as Commander of the Army of Northern Virginia as being *the* individual responsible for the identification and selection of the Confederate Officer Corps. Lee believed that the identification and selection of individuals for leadership positions was the primary function of an effective leader.

Great leaders, truly great leaders, are recognized as such because of their unique ability to connect, in a very personal way, with the people who choose to follow them. Perhaps no man understood this "connection" lesson better than General Stonewall Jackson. It is only through this personal connection that leaders earn the trust, respect, and unconditional support of those individuals they are responsible for leading—the kind of unconditional trust that manifested itself during the Civil War on July 1-3, 1863, during the battle at Gettysburg, Pennsylvania. At the end of the three days of fighting, a total of 57,225 casualties (28,000 Confederate soldiers and one-third of the Confederate Officer Corps), would be missing, wounded, dead, or captured, the most ever in a single battle in the history of the United States.

"Gettysburg became a postbellum focus of the "Lost Cause," a movement by writers such as Edward A. Pollard and Jubal Early to explain the reasons for the Confederate defeat in the war. A fundamental premise of their argument was that the South was doomed because of the overwhelming advantage in manpower and industrial might possessed by the North. However, they claim it also suffered because Robert E. Lee, who up until this time had been almost invincible, was betrayed by the failures of some of his key subordinates at Gettysburg: Ewell, for failing to seize Cemetery Hill on July 1; Stuart, for depriving Lee of his cavalry and intelligence-gathering ability, and especially Longstreet, for failing to attack on July 2 as early and as forcefully as Lee had originally intended. In this view, Gettysburg was seen as a pivotal lost opportunity, in which a decisive victory by Lee could have meant the end of the war in the Confederacy's favor."

It All Fell Apart

Lee failed. He failed in his primary role as the Commander of the Army of Northern Virginia in that he did not select a core of leaders with the necessary skills and ability to effectively lead others in battle by functioning as a team when it mattered the most. The Generals of Lee's Officer Corps failed to fully understand and appreciate the strategy of the impending battle as Lee saw it playing out. What's worse, his Generals did not completely understand and accept the role each of them was being asked to play in the conflict. For the first time in the war, Lee would experience a complete organizational failure on the part of his Office Corps. Having never seen or experienced one before, he was not able to recognize it for what it was, and by the time he did, it was already too late. Lee would go on to say after the battle, "It was all my fault, it was all my fault," and he was right. Lee had failed. Let's take a closer look at how and why.

Numerous clichés apply:

- An organization is only as strong as its weakest link.
- A team can only move at the speed of its slowest member.
- If you're not pulling together, you're pulling apart.
- Ten heads are better than one.

Normally, while these platitudes seldom have any real meaning, in the case of Lee and the Battle of Gettysburg, they are extremely relevant.

Early in the war, General Lee assembled a leadership team comprised of General Stonewall Jackson, General Jeb Stuart, and General James Longstreet. Lee often likened Stonewall Jackson to a hammer and General Longstreet to an anvil. About Stonewall Jackson, Lee would say, "Such an executive officer the sun never shone on. I have but to show him but my design, and I know that if it can be done, it will be done." Using the cavalry of General Stuart to provide Lee with timely intelligence concerning Union troop movements, Lee was able to consistently position his army to exploit any perceived Union weaknesses. The combination and coordination of the talent Lee had assembled proved highly effective at the battles of the First Bull Run, the Valley Campaign, the Peninsula Campaign, and the Battle of Fredericksburg; however, these strings of successes would all come to an end at the Battle of Chancellorsville.

At Chancellorsville, General Stonewall Jackson was mistaken as a Union soldier and shot three times by his own troops only to die eight days later from pneumonia as a result of the surgery to amputate his left arm. Upon hearing that Jackson had been wounded and that his left arm had been amputated, Lee replied, "Give General Jackson my affectionate regards, and say to him: he has lost his left arm, but I, my right."

The death of Stonewall Jackson forced Lee to restructure and expand his Officer Corps. His new team of leaders would include General James Longstreet, Jeb Stuart, Richard Ewell, George Pickett, and A. P. Hill. Lees' initial plan of attack was designed to flank the Union forces located on Culp's Hill and Cemetery Ridge in coordination with a frontal assault to be led by General Picket up Cemetery Ridge. It would be the first time this combination of leaders would work together under the new command structure. General Lee met for three days with his officers to develop their battle plan.

What Lee said to his officers and their understandings of the conversation remains hotly debated among scholars still today. What we do know is this, General Longstreet said and wrote that he did not agree with the battle plan designed by Lee. Longstreet is reported to have said, "General Lee, I have been a soldier all my life. I have been with soldiers engaged in fights by couples, by squads, companies, regiments, divisions, and armies, and should know, as well as anyone, what soldiers can do. It is my opinion that no fifteen thousand men ever arrayed for battle can take that position." In the end, for what-ever reason, Longstreet failed to meet Lee's command expectations. General Stuart, at the time his cavalry was most needed by Lee to provide him with reconnaissance and intelligence could not be found, A. P. Hill failed in his attempt to take Culp's Hill, General Ewell failed to secure Cemetery Hill, and General Picket would lead his troops straight up the slopes of Cemetery Ridge into the heart of the Union lines, as ordered, losing an estimated 6,000 men, nearly half of those involved in the failed frontal assault. Years later, when asked why his charge at Gettysburg failed, Pickett would reply: "I've always thought the Yankees had something to do with it."

Very Bad Results

- In his memoirs, General Longstreet would state publicly that Lee had never given him an order to attack, "Under no circumstances were we to give battle, but exhaust our skill in trying to force the enemy to do so in a position of our own choosing. The 1st Corps was to receive the attack and initiate the battle. The other Corps were to join the battle, fall upon the Yankees and destroy the Union Army of the Potomac."
- When General Stuart's cavalry did eventually show up at Gettysburg, it would be too late for him to make a difference in the outcome of the battle.
- General Pickett, after his ill-fated charge would be fired by General Lee and replaced a short time later. The two never reconciled, Lee believing to his death the General Picket single handedly destroyed his Division.
- On April 9, 1865, General Lee would sign the letter of surrender at Appomattox Courthouse, officially bringing about the end both the Civil War and the Confederacy

It is important to remember the history concerning Robert E. Lee. Lee graduated from West Point in 1829 and quickly distinguished himself as a Union Officer fighting in the Mexican American War of 1846 - 1848; it was the first time both Lee and Grant actually served and fought together. From 1829 to 1861, Lee had done nothing but establish a proven track record of success regarding anything he put his hand to militarily. Interestingly enough, it was Robert E. Lee who was charged with putting down the slave insurrection of 1859 at Harpers Ferry, Virginia. It is reported that under Lee's leadership, the Union Army put down the slave insurrection in under three minutes resulting in the capture of John Brown, a well-known abolitionist at the time. Brown would later be tried and executed for his actions.

Given Lee's exemplary performance as a Union military officer, in 1861 at the age of 55 immediately after the shelling of Fort Sumter, President Abraham Lincoln offered Colonel Robert E. Lee command of the combined forces of the Union Army, believing him to be the finest military leader of that time. By all accounts, Lee was a brilliant military strategist and a great leader of men. All that being said, when the battle of Gettysburg was over, and the Confederate Army lay in ruin, no longer able to continue fighting, Lee summed up the situation correctly by telling his men, "I have failed. The failure is mine." A lesser man would have falsely affixed the blame elsewhere, but not General Lee. General Robert E. Lee teaches us the most fundamental principle concerning why leadership is so critical to an organization; *because when leaders fail...bad things happen!* It is important to note that bad things don't happen to an organization for no reason; organizations fail because leadership has failed in Titanic fashion to perform their primary responsibility: to lead properly.

The challenge faced by Robert E. Lee in assembling a team of diverse personalities and getting them to function in a coordinated and unified manner continues to challenge leaders in business and industry today. Unfortunately, unlike General Lee, who was recognized as a leader with the skills and technical knowledge to engage and inspire others, many of today's leaders are completely clueless when it comes to building vibrant and dynamic organizations.

Not only do the majority of today's leaders lack the skills to lead properly, but they also lack the skills necessary to lead altogether. I always find it interesting that the worst leaders are often the ones who refuse to accept that they are the weakest link in their organizations.

It is important to remember that dysfunctional organizations do not occur by accident. Dysfunction is a natural and predictable byproduct of leadership that consistently and intentionally introduces various malignant behaviors into the organization's culture. To understand precisely what these malignant behaviors are, and the effects they have on an otherwise healthy organization, we need to turn our attention to the field of Forensic Pathology.

Forensic Leadership Pathology

Forensic Pathology is the scientific study of cause and effect. It is a highly-specialized branch of medicine that enables medical professionals to determine the specific cause of death associated with the passing of an individual. For those who are unfamiliar with the term pathology, it's the medical specialty concerned with the study of the nature and causes of diseases. In simple terms, pathology is the study of diseases.

The origins of pathology can be traced back to the Middle East during the Islamic Golden Age between the 8th and 14th centuries. Interestingly enough, the earliest know Islamic hospital was built in 805 in Bagdad under the direction of the ruler Adud al-Dawl. By 982, Bagdad would go one to build another six hospitals. Abu Bakr Muhammad ibn Zakariyya al-Razi (852-925) was the first individual to identify, through observation, the two diseases smallpox and measles.

As outlined in The Complete History of the Autopsy by Maud Campbell and Henry Robertson, (December 26, 2018 popularmechanics.com/science/health/a25633042/autopsy-history) the practice of medical autopsies date back to;

- 367 - 282 B.C. when Ptolemy I Soter, king of Egypt, champions pathological anatomy and establishes the great university and library of Alexandra. Most of the early dissections were performed on executed criminals.
- 335 - 280 B.C. Herophilus of Chalcedon, a Greek physician deemed to be the first anatomist, performs autopsies on humans and animals. He created many of the terms used in the fields of forensic medicine still in use today.
- 310 - 250 B.C. Erasistratus accurately noted that the heart prevented the backflow of the blood.
- 44 B.C. The first recorded autopsy occurs when Antistius examines Julius Caesar's body after his assassination, determining which of the 23 stab wounds proved fatal.
- A.D. 131 -201 Galen of Pergamon is the first person to correlate a patient's symptoms with what was found upon examining the affected area of the diseased.
- 1231 The first law to authorize human dissection is established under the reign of Holy Roman Emperor Fredrick II.
- 1247 Song Ci wrote *The Washing Away of Wrongs*, the first instructional manual on how to conduct medico-legal investigations, examine

corpses, and determine the time and caused death.

- 1507 Antonio Beniviende published *The Hidden Causes of Disease*.
- 1679 Theophile Bonet published Sepulchretum, a comprehensive, organized anthology discussing 3,000 autopsies and classifying the dissections by disease and symptoms.
- 1761 Giovanni Morgagni described what could be seen with the naked eye in his voluminous work entitled De Sedibus at Causis per Anatomen Indagatis (On the Seats and Causes of Diseases Investigated by Anatomy)
- 1800 French physician, Xavier Bichat, was the first person to dissect organs and analyze the tissues that comprise them.
- 1832 British Parliament passes the Anatomy Act, giving licensed doctors, and medical students the ability to dissect bodies.
- 1853 Autopsies become a mainstay in criminal investigations.
- 1936 Canadian physician Dr. Maude Abbott published Atlas of Congenital Heart Disease. This work improved our understanding of the heart's anatomy.

- 1990s Forensic photogrammetry, the idea for conducting noninvasive documentation of body surfaces using CT scans, MRIs, and 3D surface scanning is developed.

The process of becoming a Pathologist requires years of education and experience. The road to becoming a Pathologist starts with a four-year degree; pre-med students typically focus their studies in the areas of biology and chemistry. The four years in college, earning an undergraduate degree is followed by an additional four-years in medical school; pathologists are after all medical doctors. After eight years of higher education, the final step to becoming a Pathologist is serving an internship or residency lasting anywhere from three to seven years. The entire process, start to finish, to become a Pathologist can take up to fifteen years. During the entire process, Pathologists relentlessly train to prepare themselves to become experts in performing three primary functions; observation, analysis, and correlation. These fundamental skills first identified nearly three thousand years ago, serve as the cornerstone of forensic medicine still today. These three skills have a proven track record of yielding reliable and predictable results, which is why these three skills also serve as the cornerstone of Forensics Leadership Analysis.

Forensic Leadership Pathology is a study in applied leadership. It provides individuals with the skills and knowledge necessary to perform real-time Leadership Autopsies based on their ability to;

1. Observe and identify specific malignant leadership characteristics,

2. Analyze and correlate these behaviors to the organization's functional culture,

3. Reliably predict the impact existing leadership will have on an organization.

Unlike forensic medicine which requires that the individual under the knife to have shuffled off the mortal coil, kicked the bucket, or to be in the process of taking a dirt nap, a Forensic Leadership Autopsy allows us to understand the impact a leader is having on an organization in real-time; before the organization implodes from within. A Forensic Leadership Autopsy provides the tools and knowledge to recognize a leadership train-wreck long before it actually manifests in the real world; *if you know what to look for.*

Culture is What You Do!

As someone who has extensively studied and written on the subject of leadership, I have come to understand that while leaders are responsible for a great many things, the single most important job of a leader is to establish and foster a healthy organizational culture. When it comes to creating an organizational culture, leaders have only two ways to go. Either they build a healthy organizational culture that manifests a dynamic, vibrant, and robust organization, or they create a malignant organizational culture that spreads throughout the organization like the cancer it truly is, harming everyone and everything it contacts.

Great leaders have always understood that creating a healthy organizational culture is their top priority. Think of organizational culture as a verb, an action word. The "real" boots on the ground culture of an organization is always observable. This concept is so important it bears repeating. ***The real culture of an organization is always observable.*** It is precisely because the culture of an organization is always observable, through the actions of its people, that Forensic Leadership Pathology works. The following examples help illustrate this point that culture is what you do!

Cheese Heads Rule!

The Green Bay Packers have a rabid fan base—the entire state of Wisconsin. The Green Bay Packers have a long history, a proven track record, of achievement. Winning is who they are. The Packers have won thirteen league championships, the most in NFL history, with nine pre-Super Bowl National Football League titles along with four Super Bowl victories; Super Bowl I, II, XXXI and XLV, which is why Green Bay is often referred to as Title Town.

Green Bay fans are recognized for their tenacious loyalty, which results in filling Lambeau Field on even in the most frigid of football conditions. The coldest game ever played at Lambeau Field was the 1967 NFL Championship game, known as "The Ice Bowl." The temperature at game time was -13 degrees, yet the Packers played to a sold-out stadium. Rabid cheese heads fans, the Lambeau Leap, inclement weather, and winning all help define and create the Packer culture. For those unfamiliar with the Green Bay Packers, the G on their helmet does not stand for Green Bay; it stands for Greatness, which fits their culture nicely. In Green Bay, players such as Don Hutson, Bart Star, Ray Nitschke, Reggie White, Brett Favre, and Aron Rodgers, all played their part in establishing a culture of winning that helps define the Green Bay Packers.

Lobster Central

While the state of Maine is recognized for beautiful fall colors, delicious maple syrup, and J. B. Fletcher, in Maine, it's really all about the lobster. Main has become synonymous with this tasty and most delicious shellfish. A plethora of lobster houses are located throughout the state. Some of the more notable ones include: Five Island Lobster Company, Georgetown, Waterman's Beach Lobster, South Thomaston, Shaw's Fish and Lobster Restaurant in New Harbor, Estes Lobster House, Harpswell Neck, Harraseeket Lunch and Lobster in South Freeport, and finally Young's Lobster Pound in Belfast.

There are lobster rolls, freshly boiled lobster, grilled lobster, lobster shirts, lobster hats, lobster bibs, lobster costumes, lobster parades, lobster shacks, lobster fisherman, and a host of various lobster festivities such as the Rockland Lobster Festival, the Ms. Maine Lobster Queen Pageant, The York Lobster and Clam Bake, Harvest On the Harbor: Main Lobster Chef of the Year, The Brunswick Lobster Dip, Main Lobster Ride, Lobstering by Sail, the Winter Harbor Lobster Festival, Beil's Lobster Pier, the Frenchboro Lobster Festival, Harvest on the Harbor in Portland, the Maine Lobster Museum, the Lobster Institute at the University of Main, and finally National Lobster Day; celebrated in practically every lobster shack and restaurant throughout the entire state of Maine. No doubt about it, Maine embraces everything lobster because in the state of Maine, lobster is simply what they do!

All About the Beer

Few countries are associated with and take greater pride in being recognized for all things related to beer, as does Germany. There are over 1,300 breweries in Germany that produce over 5,000 brands of beer annually. The highest density of breweries in the world is found in Aufseß near the city of Bamberg, in the Franconia region of Bavaria, with four breweries and only 1,352 citizens.

Germany produces approximately 94.96 million hectoliters of beer annually, which comes in handy, because per capita, Germans consume 28 gallons of beer annually. This makes them one of the top three beer-drinking countries in Europe. Germany produces so many different beers that an individual could drink a different beer every day for fifteen years before having to drink the same beer twice. That's a lot of beer!

Perhaps nothing illustrates the German love for beer better than October Fest. October Fest is the world's largest beer festival held annually in Munich, Germany.

Octoberfest is a 16 - 18 day folk festival running from mid or late September to the first Sunday in October. More than six million people from around the world attend this event every year. During Octoberfest, some 6 million visitors will consume nearly 8 million liters of beer, 72% of which is brewed in Bavaria.

Beer, beer gardens, beer halls, beer barrels, beer steins, Stout, Malt, Ale, Pilsner, and Lagers all work together to define the German culture because, in Germany, beer is what they do!

Idaho & Potatoes

The great state of Idaho is recognized around the world for having some of the world's most beautiful rivers, filled with thirty-inch rainbow and cutthroat trout that attract fishermen from all around the world. Seventy percent on the state is wilderness, completely void of any public roads or electricity. Evil Knievel failed in his attempt to jump the Snake River near Twin Falls, Idaho. Each year Boise State carries on the tradition of being the team few NCAA Division I schools want to play. Yet all of this pales in comparison to the greatness of the humble Russet potato. In Idaho, the potato is king!

Famous Idaho potatoes dominate just about every aspect of the state, The NCAA Boise Potato Bowl, Simplot, French fries, tater tots, hash browns, funeral potatoes, (it's a local thing, but incredibly delicious), potato bars, potato soup, potato bread, baked potatoes, stuffed potatoes, twice baked potatoes, mashed potatoes, potato skins, potato pancakes, potato hash, potato salad, potato chips, potato waffles, potato au gratin, potato harvest, potato barns, potato pizza, Spudnik, Idaho Spud Day, Miss Idaho Potato Queen, the famous Idaho potato truck, the Potato Museum located in Blackfoot, ID and of course, the very famous and stylish poster of Marilyn Monroe wearing the ever comfortable and popular burlap potato sack.

I will never forget my surprise when I ordered tacos from a local restaurant in American Falls, Idaho, only to find mixed in with the taco meat an equal portion of diced potatoes. Coming from Arizona, I found the potato filling a bit odd, but to the locals, they could not imagine a taco made any other way.

In Idaho, potatoes are celebrated in everything they do. The humble tuber is present in just about every social gathering. Potato farming drives seventy percent of the state's economy, which is why, in Idaho, potatoes are what they do!

Holiday Travel

One final example. Every Holiday Season, millions of Americans travel thousands of miles so they can be home for the holidays. In November 2016, it was estimated 44 million Americans traveled home for the Thanksgiving holiday. AAA estimates that in 2016 roughly 103 million Americans traveled home for Christmas. In America, the need for family members to gather together during the Holiday Season has always been a defining characteristic of our nation. The Rockwellian image of families coming together to celebrate holidays together captures the very essence of our national culture in action.

Norman Rockwell's painting, Christmas Homecoming, provides for us a wonderful and heartwarming reminder of who we are, because in America, coming together as families during the Holiday Season is simply what we do.

I use these examples to help explain a fundamental principle that serves as the cornerstone of Forensic Leadership Pathology, that *culture is nothing more than what we do!* This concept is essential to understand because it is absolutely rejected by failing and or dysfunctional leaders. Failing, malignant leaders choose to believe that what they do, that their actions are neither reflective of them as an individual, or the organization they are responsible for leading; it's how they continue to justify their malignant behaviors, but more on that later.

Forensic Leadership Pathology enables us to better understand and predict an organization's future based on the current actions of its leadership. Since organizational culture is nothing more than the fruition of a leader's actions, by paying attention to how leaders conduct themselves publicly and privately, by observing how leaders treat others, how leaders behave under pressure, by observing what policies and procedures the leader fosters and enforces, how and what message a leaders communicates through actions, and what values a leader promotes, a Forensic Leadership Pathologist can become highly skilled in identifying broken organizations and the malignant leaders who are responsible for breaking them.

It is important to remember when it comes to evaluating leadership; a leader's actions are the only things that matter. A leader's actions are the ultimate litmus test of who they are and what they value. Their actions provide the most reliable insight concerning the ethical values and internal motivation that drives them as individuals. Four excellent examples of this include;

- Leona Helmsley, the "Queen of Mean." A self-made billionaire in the hotel and real-estate business, on August 30, 1989, "Leona Helmsley was convicted of one count of conspiracy to defraud the United States, three counts of tax evasion, three counts of filing false personal tax returns, sixteen counts of assisting in the filing of false corporate and partnership tax returns, and ten counts of mail fraud," (Wikipedia January 1, 2020). Leona Helmsley was driven by money, making it, acquiring it, keeping it, and above all, making sure no-one else got any of it; for any reason.

- Carlos Ghosn, the ex-Nissan CEO, "Ghosn, out on bail in Tokyo in late 2019, is facing criminal charges including under-reporting his salary and abusing his position by transferring personal investment losses to Nissan." (CNN Business, October 2020). After posting nearly $13,000,000 in bail, and turning over numerous passports, Mr. Ghosn fled Japan and made his way safely to Lebanon, a nation where he holds dual citizenship. In a statement to the press concerning his departure Carlos Ghosn is reported to have said, he has "not fled justice, I have escaped injustice and political persecution." We may never know the truth surrounding Carlos Ghosn; however, we can observe his actions, which appear to lack any semblance of integrity and or meaningful transparency.

- David Howell Petraeus, Retired U.S. General and past Director of the Central Intelligence Agency. "In January 2015, officials reported the FBI and Justice Department prosecutors had recommended bringing felony charges against Petraeus for allegedly providing classified information to his biographer, Paula Broadwell (with whom he was having an affair) while serving as Director of the CIA. Eventually, Petraeus pleaded guilty to one misdemeanor charge of mishandling classified information" (Wikipedia 2020). As a graduate of West Point and a Retired General, he was more than vaguely familiar with the West Point motto, "Duty, Honor, Country." However, in the end, his West Point training and education did not serve as the guiding principles that actually governed his actions.

- In January 2020, Boeing fired its CEO, Dennis Muilenburg. The actual events leading up to his termination are truly tragic. "Lion Air Flight 610 took off from Jakarta, Indonesia, on Monday, October 29th, 2018, at 6:20 a.m. local time. Its destination was Bangkal Pinang, the largest city of Indonesia's Bangkal Belitung Islands. Twelve minutes after takeoff, the plane crashed into the Java Sea, killing all 189 passengers and crew. Nearly five months later, Ethiopian Airlines Flight 302 took off from Addis Ababa, Ethiopia, on Sunday, March 10th, 2019, at 8:38 a.m. local time. Its destination was Nairobi, Kenya. Six minutes after takeoff, the plane crashed near the town of Bishoftu, Ethiopia, killing all 157 people aboard." (The Verge). A total of 346 people lost their lives as a result of software that literally flew two planes into the ground. In their investigation of the two crashes, the FAA would later discover that Boeing's leadership had been made aware of the problem. The New York Times would go on to report, "Boeing's chief technical pilot on the 737 Max project told another employee in 2016 that there were "egregious" problems with the jet's automated anti-stall system, two years before the first of two fatal crashes attributed to the system." In the end, the legacy of 737 MAX and the leadership of Dennis Muilenburg would show that ***based on their actions*** the Boeing culture of putting safety first, was no longer the company's guiding principle. Under the leadership of Muilenburg and the Boeing Board of Directors, Boeings' leadership modeled a new corporate value; its name was profit.

These extremely powerful and influential individuals all serve as excellent reminders that when leadership fails, bad things happen. It's important to remember that each of these individuals acted poorly in their leadership roles. Each of these individuals possessed the trappings of leadership; they had the right titles, they held prominent and influential positions, hundreds, and in some cases, thousands of individuals reported to them, they each had decision making authority, and financially they were all compensated handsomely. However, in the end, each of them failed in their primary responsibility as a leader; to lead properly.

Houston, We Have a Problem!

Show me a dysfunctional organization, and I'll show you a malignant leader. Death by Leadership is not a book about how to fix malignant dysfunctional leaders. Dysfunctional leaders are seldom interested in making any personal change primarily because their leadership style works perfectly well for them. It may not serve the needs of anybody else, but it has allowed these individuals to climb the ladder of success, and now that they find themselves on the top rung, they are not about to fix what is working perfectly well for them.

The purpose of this book is to provide you with the skills and knowledge to become a Forensic Leadership Pathologist so that you can avoid these individuals. To do this, you will need to become confident in your ability to observe an organization's culture in action, analyze the drivers of this behavior, and finally correlate these established institutional behaviors to predictive and highly probable long-term outcomes. Forensic Leadership Pathologists are skilled in their abilities to observe, analyze, and predict because it is precisely these skills which serve as the cornerstone of Forensic Leadership Pathology.

Leadership Autopsy Toe Tag

Just as Medical Examiners must master a new vocabulary of medical terminology to identify, synthesize and effectively communicate their understanding of the events leading up to the death of a decedent, a Forensic Leadership Pathologist must be equally well versed in the following thirteen, very specific, malignant leadership characteristics so that they can readily identify, analyze and clearly articulate their findings concerning the overall capabilities and fitness of the leader they are evaluating. Consequently, the rest of our time will be dedicated to discussing the thirteen malignant behaviors which make up a Leadership Autopsy Toe Tag.

Forensic Leadership Analysis ™.			
Evaluator:			
Organization:			
Leadership Autopsy Toe Tag ™			
Instructions: Check "Yes" if behavior is observable. Check "No" if the behavior is not observable. If behavior is present, circle Value. Add all circled scores together to generate a total score. Compare total score to Evaluation Scale.			
Malignant Behaviors	Observed **Yes**	Value	Observed **No**
Lying		6	
Hubris		6	
Avarice		6	
Duplicity		6	
Cunning		5	
Narcissism		5	
Disconnection		5	
Deception		4	
Dismissiveness		4	
Manipulation		4	
Inconsistency		3	
Unteachability		3	
Gamesmanship		3	
	Total Score		
Evaluation Scale	**Levels**		**Action**
Score 40 - 60	Dying Organization		**Run!**
Score 21 - 39	Malignancy Spreading		**Update Resume**
Score 1 - 20	Malignancy Present		**Observe Closely**

For Forensic Leadership Pathologists to accurately perform a Leadership Autopsy, they must possess a clear and precise understanding of the specific malignant leadership behaviors frequently modeled by failing leadership. To foster the universal adoption of the Forensic Leadership Autopsy vernacular, we will rely heavily on Webster's Dictionary as our source document to establish the working definition of the terms which comprise the Leadership Autopsy Toe Tag.

I want to be very clear. You do not have to have a Doctorate, MBA, or Master's Degree to be a Forensic Leadership Pathologist. You are not required to have experience as a Board Member, CEO, President, Vice-President, Regional Manager, District Manager, General Manager, or possess any title what-so-ever to become skilled as a Forensic Leadership Pathologist capable of a performing a meaningful and relevant Leadership Autopsy. Being a Forensic Leadership Pathologist requires common sense, confidence, and conviction in your ability to observe accurately and objectively, and finally, an ethical grounding that enables you to tell the difference between right and wrong. Forensic Leadership Pathologists are instilled with a fundamental ethical underpinning which prepares them to understand the difference between right and wrong when they see it in action.

It should not come as a surprise that failing, malignant leaders, reject the notion that trained and informed Forensic Leadership Pathologists possess the skills or ability to evaluate their influence or impact as leaders. Malignant leaders tend to insist that what they do is so complicated, requires such unique skills, talent, and knowledge, that no one, besides themselves, is capable of evaluating or judging their leadership performance.

The idea that leaders cannot be accurately evaluated by a trained Forensic Leadership Pathologist is complete and utter hogwash! Fortunately, individuals trained in Forensic Leadership Pathology possess the skills and knowledge to look beyond the superficial, the smoke and mirrors, to observe and identify what really matters.

Definition of Terms

So, what exactly is malignant leadership?

Malignant: adjective

Definition:

1. disposed to cause harm, suffering, or distress deliberately; feeling or showing ill will or hatred.
2. very dangerous or harmful in influence or effect.

When something is malignant, that means sooner or later it's more than likely going to cause harm, malignancy is inherently a very bad thing. Think of it like cancer. Most people understand that cancer, in general, is a bad thing; it's not something most people would willingly choose to introduce into their bodies. Malignant leadership is exactly like cancer. Ultimately, a malignant leader's behaviors will have the same impact on the organization they infuse with it as cancer cells do on healthy tissue. Fortunately, identifying malignant leadership is not difficult if you know what to look for.

Malignant Leadership is comprised of thirteen highly dysfunctional leadership characteristics or behaviors: Lying, Hubris, Avarice, Duplicity, Cunning, Narcissism, Disconnection, Deception, Dismissiveness, Manipulation, Inconsistency, Unteachability, and Gamesmanship.

There are two very important things to understand about malignant leadership. First, malignant leadership will ultimately destroy the very organization they are responsible for leading. It not a question of if, it's a question when. Second, the impact these malignant behaviors have on an organization grows exponentially relative to the number of malignant behaviors they introduce into the organization. In simple terms, the more malignant behaviors a leader introduces into an organization the faster that organization becomes dysfunctional and dies. Organizational dysfunction is even further exacerbated when malignant leaders surround themselves with like-minded individuals. Perhaps you are familiar with the old saying, "birds of a feather flock together." This is absolutely the case when it comes to malignant leaders. You may notice in our case studies that it is common for malignant leaders to introduce multiple malignant behaviors into an organization. In those instances, you will observe a significant correlation between the number of observable malignant behaviors and the degree, or severity, of organizational dysfunction.

Be aware; when something is malignant, that means sooner or later, it's going to destroy whatever it is attached to. Malignant leadership is no different; ultimately cancerous malignant behaviors will destroy even the healthiest and most profitable organization.

While any of the thirteen malignant leadership characteristics are harmful and disruptive to the people and organizations affected by them, not all malignant behaviors are equal. Some malignant characteristics, in and of themselves, are more destructive than others. Consequently, we will begin a definition of terms, starting with absolutely horrific malignant leadership practices and conclude with the more garden variety of simply horrible malignant leadership characteristics.

13 Malignant Leadership Characteristics

Malignant Leadership Characteristic #1 ***Lying***

Lying: noun

Definition:

Marked by or containing untrue statements.

Examples of *lying* include the following;

President William Jefferson Clinton

"I did not have sexual relations with that woman."

President Lyndon B. Johnson

"We are not about to send American boys nine or ten thousand miles away from home to do what Asian boys ought to be doing for themselves."

President Richard Milhous Nixon

"I am not a crook. And in all of my years of public life I have never obstructed justice."

President Donald John Trump

"In addition to winning the Electoral College in a landslide, I won the popular vote if you deduct the millions of people who voted illegally."

All of the above statements have the same thing in common; they are all marked by or contain untrue statements. As we now know, President Clinton did have sexual relations with that woman, President Johnson did send American troops to Vietnam, President Nixon did obstruct justice, and President Trump did not win the popular vote. Each of these leaders lied. When it comes to lying, it's a case of black or white; you either tell the truth, the whole truth, and nothing but the truth or you don't. It is never a bit of both.

Why It Matters

Lying destroys all trust. When leaders no longer have the confidence of the individuals they are responsible for leading, they can no longer be effective leaders. Trust is the glue that binds people and healthy organizations together. When trust exists, all things are possible, when trust is absent, failure is eminent.

I am familiar with leaders who routinely fail to honor any agreement they did not "put in writing." I have known leaders who had difficulty honoring written contracts, insisting instead that everything needed to be continually re-negotiated to reflect current market conditions.

Observe how a leader conducts business. Observe how a leader directs others to conduct business as well. Do they encourage individuals within the organization to act unethically? Do they reward individuals for inappropriate, abusive, unethical, and or border-line criminal activity?

There are endless examples of leaders who routinely make up facts as they need them. Unfortunately, there are leaders in the public and private sectors whose only concern is themselves and making themselves look good at all costs. To that end, if they have to stretch a few truths, tell a few harmless white lies, or fabricate a whole new alternate reality, so be it; no harm, no foul.

The litmus Test

Warren Buffet is famous for saying, "Lose money for the firm, and I will be understanding. Lose a shred of reputation for the firm, and I will be ruthless." When leaders lie, they destroy the reputation of the people and organization they are responsible for leading.

Key Points

When people realize and accept that their leadership is not in the habit of telling the truth, lying inevitably becomes the dominant culture throughout the organization. Individuals learn to model the art of misdirection, omission, exaggeration, or complete fabrication as a direct result of seeing their leadership not only practice but condone these same behaviors by others.

As a Forensic Leadership Pathologist, when you recognize that a leader is not truthful in dealings with others, you have successfully identified the first malignant behavior on the Leadership Toe Tag.

Forensic Leadership Analysis ™.			
Evaluator:			
Organization:			
Leadership Autopsy Toe Tag ™			
Instructions: Check "Yes" if behavior is observable. Check "No" if the behavior is not observable. If behavior is present, circle Value. Add all circled scores together to generate a total score. Compare total score to Evaluation Scale.			
Malignant Behaviors	Observed **Yes**	Value	Observed **No**
Lying	✓	6	

Example:

Lying identified as "Observed" on a Leadership Autopsy Toe Tag

Malignant Leadership Characteristic #2 ***Hubris***

Hubris: noun

Definition:

Exaggerated pride or self-confidence.

Examples of hubris include the following;

General Douglas McArthur

On June 25, 1950, North Korea invaded South Korea; this would be the beginning of the Korean conflict. On July 8, 1950, on the advice on the Joint Chiefs of Staff, President Truman appointed General Douglas MacArthur as commander of the United Nations Command in South Korea (CINCUNC). It was probably the first and last thing these two men would ever agree on. MacArthur did not agree with President Truman's handling of the situation and made numerous public comments, which were extremely critical of President Truman. Those comments would ultimately lead to his firing. President Truman would later say, "I fired him because he wouldn't respect the authority of the President. I didn't fire him because he was a dumb son of a bitch, although he was, but that's not against the law for generals. If it was, half to three-quarters of them would be in jail."

Ms. Carly Fiorina

Carley Fiorina was the CEO and Chairman of Hewlett Packard. She was dismissed for performance-related issues in 2005 but received $45 million, including a $21 million severance package. Under her leadership, in three and a half years, HP lost half its market value and laid off thirty thousand employees while at the same time managed to update its fleet of corporate jets.

In her book, *Tough Choices*, Fiorina would go on to say, "In the end, the board did not have the courage to face me," she goes on to say, "They did not thank me, and they did not say good-bye." What Fiorina may have lacked in leadership, she more than compensated for in hubris.

President Donald Trump

On June 12, 2018, at a NATO press conference, President Donald Trump proclaimed, "I'm a very stable genius."

The individuals in these examples all share a common characteristic, an extremely over-inflated ego. They model, in how they comport themselves, an exaggerated sense of pride, and or self-importance.

Why It Matters

It is safe to say that as the Supreme Leader of North Korea, Kim Jong-un has no rivals. One reason is that as The Supreme Leader Kim Jong-un has a well-earned reputation for quickly eliminating any threats, real or perceived. According to the news source The Telegraph, "Kim Jong-un, the North Korean dictator, reportedly ordered the execution of his uncle and mentor in December 2013 after learning that Jang Song-thaek had proposed to China that it support a coup to replace Mr. Kim with his half-brother, Kim Jong-nam," (The Telegraph, August 2017). Kim Jong-un also put to death members of Jang's family, to completely destroy all traces of Jang's existence through "extensive executions" of his family, including the children and grandchildren of all close relatives.

When leaders embrace hubris, they typically have a skewed perception of the people close to them, falsely believing the individuals they are responsible for leading pose threats to their authority or position within the organization. Ironically, the more talented, capable, and competent an individual is, the greater the threat they pose to leaders governed by hubris.

A Litmus Test

Because hubris leaders typically see themselves as the most important people in the organization, they are fairly easy to recognize simply by listening to them as they speak about themselves and their accomplishments. Start by observing who a leader talks about most. Observe who a leader acknowledges for contributing to the success of the organization. Listen to who they praise. Watch who the leader rewards for performance. If you observe that the leader sees themselves as the nexus of the organization, only recognizing their accomplishments, constantly congratulating themselves publicly, or carefully orchestrating event so others can publicly praise them, you have successfully identified the presence of Hubris in the organization you are evaluating.

Key Points

The key to a healthy and vibrant organization are the many talented individuals who comprise it. Malignant leaders who allow hubris to govern their actions will naturally and predictably drive the best, the brightest, and the most capable individuals away. Leaders who embrace hubris must be the center of attention at all times, which is why they habitually drive equally talented people away. Hubris leaders deserve and demand all credit because in their minds everything is always about them. The most popular words in a hubris leader's vocabulary are the words I, me, and my.

As a Forensic Leadership Pathologist, when you observe a leader who continually praise themselves for their own performance, you have successfully identified the malignancy of hubris in action.

Forensic Leadership Analysis TM.			
Evaluator:			
Organization:			
Leadership Autopsy Toe Tag TM			
Instructions: Check "Yes" if behavior is observable. Check "No" if the behavior is not observable. If behavior is present, circle Value. Add all circled scores together to generate a total score. Compare total score to Evaluation Scale.			
Malignant Behaviors	Observed **Yes**	Value	Observed **No**
Hubris	✓	6	

Example:

Hubris identified as "Observed" on a Leadership Autopsy Toe Tag

Malignant Leadership Characteristic #3 ***Avarice***

Avarice: noun

Definition:

Excessive or insatiable desire for wealth or gain.

Examples of avarice include the following;

For those familiar with the 60s TV show The Beverly Hillbillies, Mr. Drysdale provides us with an excellent example of avarice at work. As far as Milburn Drysdale was concerned, it was not possible to ever have too much money.

Charles Dickens' character Ebenezer Scrooge in the Christmas Carol epitomizes what it means to live a life of avarice. Scrooge placed his love for money above all else. When you think of avarice, think of Scrooge.

Jordan Belfort, the Wolf of Wall Street, serves as an excellent example of what happens when a leader embraces avarice. "In 1999, he pleaded guilty to fraud and related crimes in connection with stock market manipulation and running a boiler room as part of a penny stock scam.

> Belfort spent 22 months in prison as part of an agreement under which he gave testimony against numerous partners and subordinates in his fraud scheme," (Wikipedia, 2020). Belfort had a well-earned reputation for his lavish lifestyle and extravagant excesses. No amount of money or extravagance was ever enough.

The individuals in these examples all share a common characteristic, an insatiable need for more, more money, more power, more prestige, more fame, no amount of whatever they craved could possibly be enough. Mary Trump succinctly captures the very essence of avarice in the title of her new book, "Too Much and Never Enough."

Why It Matters

Leaders who embrace avarice typically align organizational resources to fulfill their personal needs and desires, needs which can never be satiated regardless of how much they receive. Individuals working in organizations whose leadership embraces avarice often find themselves constantly competing for consistently declining financial resources. Leaders who embrace avarice often mis-direct organizational financial resources on themselves, not the organization they are responsible for serving, not the people doing the work or providing the service and certainly not on the organization as a whole. All recognition and rewards are designed and structured to satisfy the needs and wants of leadership. For example, at the same time the CEO of Hewlett Packard (HP) found it necessary to fire 35,000 employees to reduce operating costs, she was upgrading the HP fleet of corporate jets to make travel more enjoyable and convenient for the leadership of the organization.

A Litmus Test

Avarice indicators are neither difficult nor challenging to spot. Look for signs of excessive spending, especially in the areas of CEO performance bonuses, multi-million-dollar stock options based on performance indicators, perks such as unlimited use of corporate jets, corporate luxury condos, corporate chefs, yachts, luxury homes, and low or no interest loan options. When determining whether or not a leader is driven by avarice, look at how well they share their toys with others.

As a Forensic Leadership Pathologist, when you observe a leader who acts as if they not only own all the toys in the sandbox, but the sandbox itself, you will have successfully identified the malignancy of avarice in action.

Forensic Leadership Analysis ™.			
Evaluator:			
Organization:			
Leadership Autopsy Toe Tag ™			
Instructions: Check "Yes" if behavior is observable. Check "No" if the behavior is not observable. If behavior is present, circle Value. Add all circled scores together to generate a total score. Compare total score to Evaluation Scale.			
Malignant Behaviors	Observed **Yes**	Value	Observed **No**
Avarice	✓	6	

Example:
Avarice identified as "Observed" on a Leadership Autopsy Toe Tag

Malignant Leadership Characteristic #4 ***Duplicity***

Duplicity: noun

Definition:

Contradictory doubleness of thought, speech, or action.

Examples of duplicity include the following;

The Godfather, "Never tell anyone outside the family what you are thinking."

Wells Fargo was duplicitous when they created over 2,000,000 fake accounts in order to falsely inflate the institutions' number of accounts, which in turn impacted stock values.

WASHINGTON — President Trump's former national security adviser, Michael T. Flynn, pleaded guilty to lying to the F.B.I. about conversations with the Russian ambassador, becoming the first senior White House official to cut a cooperation deal in the special counsel's wide-ranging inquiry into election interference.

"I recognize that the actions I acknowledged in court today were

> wrong, and, through my faith in God, I am working to set things right," Mr. Flynn said. "My guilty plea and agreement to cooperate with the special counsel's office reflect a decision I made in the best interests of my family and of our country. I accept full responsibility for my actions." (https://www.nytimes.com/2017/12/01/us/politics/michael-flynn-guilty-russia-investigation.html)

Former national security adviser Michael Flynn asked a federal judge for permission to withdraw his guilty plea of lying to the FBI in special counsel Robert S. Mueller III's probe of Russian election interference, alleging that prosecutors breached his cooperation agreement by demanding his false testimony. (https://www.washingtonpost.com/local/legal-issues/michael-flynn-moves-to-withdraw-guilty-plea-claiming-goverment-vindictiveness/2020/01/14/f6a61b98-3736-11ea-bb7b-265f4554af6d_story.html)

Adolph Hitler, May 1935, "Nobody in this Germany, nobody in this unified and disciplined State wants war. Moreover, nobody here will take any step to cause war."

Why it Matters

Duplicity erodes the possibility of any open, honest communications. Organizations, and especially the people in those organizations who are not able to communicate honestly, are destined to fail. For an organization to prosper, everyone in that organization must have a clear understanding of where the organization is headed, what their specific role is in advancing the organization, and what ultimate success looks like so everyone will know when it has been achieved. By introducing duplicity into an organization, a leader is sowing the seeds of mistrust and internal dysfunction. Healthy organizations naturally grow because everyone in the organization shares a common vision, Malignant duplicitous leaders lack the ability to create a unifying vision. In its absence, chaos becomes the new normal as organizations stagnate.

A Litmus Test

Duplicitous leaders have a natural tendency to articulate being for and against something at the same time. Their message is designed to modulate with whatever group they are speaking to at the time; which is why duplicitous leaders are just as likely to say, "I never said that," as easily as, "I say it all the time," because, in truth, they consistently do both.

As a Forensic Leadership Pathologist, when you recognize that a leaders actions are incongruous with their words, you have successfully identified the malignant behavior of duplicity in action.

Forensic Leadership Analysis TM.			
Evaluator:			
Organization:			
Leadership Autopsy Toe Tag TM			
Instructions: Check "Yes" if behavior is observable. Check "No" if the behavior is not observable. If behavior is present, circle Value. Add all circled scores together to generate a total score. Compare total score to Evaluation Scale.			
Malignant Behaviors	Observed **Yes**	Value	Observed **No**
Duplicity	✓	6	

Example:
Duplicity identified as "Observed" on a leadership Autopsy Toe Tag

Malignant Leadership Characteristic #5 ***Cunning***

Cunning: noun

Definition :

Dexterous or crafty in the use of special resources (such as skill or knowledge) in attaining an end. Employing trickery.

Examples of cunning include the following;

Watergate, on June 17, 1972, five men broke into the DNC headquarters at the Watergate complex. When the FBI investigated the break-in, they discovered a connection between cash found on the burglars and a slush fund used by the Committee to the Re-Election of the President, the official organization of President Nixon's campaign. An investigation into the break-in revealed that President Nixon had a tape-recording system in his office that he had used to record his conversations. These records would reveal that Nixon had attempted to cover up activities that took place after the break-in as well as his attempt to use federal officials to deflect the investigation.

Bernie Madoff, on March 12, 2009, Madoff pleaded guilty to eleven federal felonies and admitted to turning his wealth management business into a massive Ponzi scheme. The Madoff investment scandal defrauded thousands of investors out of billions of dollars.

Governor Blagojevich of Illinois was arrested at his home by federal agents on December 9, 2008 and charged with corruption. The Justice Department complaint alleged that the governor conspired to commit several "pay to play" schemes, including attempting "to obtain personal gain ... through the corrupt use" of his authority to fill the United States Senate seat vacated by Barak Obama following his election as president, claiming that in wiretapped recordings, Blagojevich discussed his desire to get something in exchange for an appointment to the seat. (https://en.wikipedia.org/wiki/Rod_Blagojevich)

Why it Matters

If history teaches us anything, it is leaders who embrace the malignancy of cunning only have your back for one reason, so that when the time is right, they can stick a knife in it. Cunning leaders are deceptive, misleading, untrustworthy, and totally self-centered. They have only one concern, advancing their own careers or self-interests. Cunning leaders do not make decisions that are in the best interest of others or the organization they are responsible for leading. Cunning leaders are inherently untrustworthy.

Litmus Test

Leaders who embrace cunning lack the ability to trust others, which in turn fosters a culture of paranoia because cunning leaders believe everyone is out to get them. Cunning leaders tend to go through executives at the same rate fast food restaurants go through napkins.

As a Forensic Leadership Pathologist, when you identify leaders who thinks they are smarter than everyone else, act like they are smarter than everyone else, and need a revolving door in the Human Resource Department, congratulations, you have identified the malignancy of cunning in action.

Forensic Leadership Analysis ™.			
Evaluator:			
Organization:			
Leadership Autopsy Toe Tag ™			
Instructions: Check "Yes" if behavior is observable. Check "No" if the behavior is not observable. If behavior is present, circle Value. Add all circled scores together to generate a total score. Compare total score to Evaluation Scale.			
Malignant Behaviors	Observed **Yes**	Value	Observed **No**
Cunning	✓	5	

Example:

Cunning identified as "Observed" on a Leadership Autopsy Toe Tag

Malignant Leadership Characteristic #6 ***Narcissism***

Narcissism: noun

Definition:

Egoism, Egocentrism; excessive interest in oneself and concern for one's welfare or advantage at the expense of, or in disregard of others.

Examples of narcissism include the following;

Narcissism is the pursuit of gratification from vanity or egotistic admiration of one's idealized self-image and attributes. This includes self-flattery, perfectionism, and arrogance. The term originated from Greek mythology, where the young Narcissus fell in love with his own image reflected in a pool of water. After seeing his reflection in the water, Narcissus was so self-absorbed and drawn to his own image in the water that he drowned staring at himself (Wikipedia 2020).

General Douglas MacArthur "I have returned!" Make no doubt about it, General Douglas MacArthur saw himself as the most important man in the room, and it did not matter who was in the room with him.

For those who are familiar with the movie Dodge Ball: A True Underdog Story, the character White Goodman provides us with an excellent example of what it means to be narcissistic. For White Goodman, the world and everything in it revolved around him.

The movie, Wolf of Wall Street, serves an excellent example of narcissism at work. In this movie, Leonardo DiCaprio takes us into the life of Jordan Belfort, a New Your stockbroker and founder of Stratton Oakmont. The story of Jordan Belfort's quest to satiate his needs at the expense of others, serves as an excellent example of what happens when narcissistic leaders are allowed to run unchecked.

What it Matters

Narcissistic leaders are completely self-absorbed individuals unable to see a bigger picture or any picture for that matter, that does not have them in the center of it. Narcissistic leaders must be the center of attention at all times! Narcissistic leaders genuinely believe that every achievement obtained by their organization is not only a direct reflection, but a byproduct of their leadership. Consequently, all praise and recognition should deservedly be directed toward them and them alone. It is important to note than narcissistic leaders generally do not build strong, dynamic, and empowered organizations because anyone who threatens to take any credit for the success of the organization, no matter how minor, is quickly eliminated.

A Litmus Test

Leaders who embrace the malignancy of narcissism are not able to acknowledge and recognize the contribution of others. They often believe that they alone deserve full credit, recognition, or rewards for any success achieved by the organization. Any good ideas were their ideas.

As a Forensic Leadership Pathologist, when you hear a leader start every sentence with the word "I," followed closely by "my" and finish whatever they are saying by reminding everyone present how smart and talented they are, congratulations, you have identified the malignancy of narcissism in action.

Forensic Leadership Analysis TM.			
Evaluator:			
Organization:			
Leadership Autopsy Toe Tag TM			
Instructions: Check "Yes" if behavior is observable. Check "No" if the behavior is not observable. If behavior is present, circle Value. Add all circled scores together to generate a total score. Compare total score to Evaluation Scale.			
Malignant Behaviors	Observed **Yes**	Value	Observed **No**
Narcissism	✓	5	

Example:
Narcissism identified as "Observed" on a Leadership Autopsy Toe Tag

Malignant Leadership Characteristic #7 ***Disconnection***

Disconnection: noun

Definition:

The severed connection of or between.

Examples of disconnection include the following;

The Godfather, "It's not personal; it's business."

Marie Antionette, "Let them eat cake."

Anthony Bryan Hayward, British Petroleum Chief Executive responsible for and in the midst of the Deepwater Horizon oil spill catastrophe is reported to have said, "We're sorry for the massive disruption it's caused to their lives. There's no one who wants this thing over more than I do, I'd like my life back."

Dr. Lawrence H. Summers, President Harvard University January 17, 2005, sparked an uproar at an academic conference when he said that innate differences between men and women might be one reason fewer women succeed in science and math careers.

President Trump, March 2020, in response to significant deficiencies in the ability to provide coronavirus testing nation-wide, "I take no responsibility what-so-ever."

Why It Matters

If the popular television show Under Cover Boss serves no other purpose, it provides us with a greater understanding concerning the magnitude and scope of leaders who are completely disconnected from the organizations they are responsible for leading. The premise of the show is simple; each week, a different CEO realizes that something in their company is not working and the need for the CEO to find out why. The only way for the CEO to find out, first-hand, what is going on in their own company is to go undercover. Going undercover consists of:

1. CEO's lying to their employees about who they are and what they are doing.
2. Employing duplicity to keep everyone they meet confused as to their real intent.
3. Relying on their cunning to deceive and trick those individuals with whom they come in contact.

4. Considering themselves (narcissism) as the only person capable of fixing the problem(s).
5. Practicing the art of deception requires many of these individuals to wear costumes to hide their identity.
6. Manipulating the system and environment to fit their needs.
7. Being incredibly inconsistent in how they engage with their employees.
8. Turning the entire process into a game with winners and losers to be determined by the CEO at the end of the show.

The Litmus Test

As a Forensic Leadership Pathologist, if you want to observe a textbook example of what a disconnected leader looks like in practice, tune in to CBS and watch Undercover Boss. These leaders provide us with real-world examples of the malignancy of disconnection in action.

Forensic Leadership Analysis TM.			
Evaluator:			
Organization:			
Leadership Autopsy Toe Tag TM			
Instructions: Check "Yes" if behavior is observable. Check "No" if the behavior is not observable. If behavior is present, circle Value. Add all circled scores together to generate a total score. Compare total score to Evaluation Scale.			
Malignant Behaviors	Observed **Yes**	Value	Observed **No**
Disconnection	✓	5	

Example:
Disconnection identified as "Observed" on a Leadership Autopsy Toe Tag

Malignant Leadership Characteristic #8 ***Deception***

Deception: noun

Definition:

The act of causing someone to accept as true or valid what is false or invalid: the act of deceiving.

Examples of deception include the following;

Charles Ponzi, born on March 3, 1882, a swindler and con artist, will forever be remembered for perfecting the Ponzi scheme. His specialty was in deceiving individuals into investing their money into his fraudulent investment schemes. By the time it all finally collapsed on November 1, 1920, Charles Ponzi would cheat his clients out of $20 million dollars, roughly $211 million by today's standards.

Jeff Skilling, CEO of Enron, and his established practice of Market to Market Accounting was deceptive in both its design and implementation. When Enron signed a long-term contract to provide power out of a new power plant still under construction, they immediately recorded all profits estimated to be made under the contract. On paper, this made Enron look like an incredibly financially sound company to invest in when in reality, Enron was hemorrhaging money. Imagine the false perception Skilling could create concerning Enron's financial position by posting/claiming hypothetical as opposed to actual income? Enron would end up declaring bankruptcy impacting shareholders some $74 billion dollars.

Crazy Eddie was a retail store located in the Northeastern United States in the early 70s. At the time, the store achieved national notoriety for the Crazy Eddie ads they ran on TV. The ads always started out saying, "Crazy Eddie is so crazy…." In 1980 Eddie decided to take the company public. In efforts to drive the value of his now publicly held stock up, he needed to show two things, strong sales, and a large inventory. To inflate his inventory, Eddie continued to warehouse and inventory all the empty boxes from the merchandise he had sold. Eddie also introduced the world to "The Panama Pump," a cash infusion scheme designed to inflate revenue and manipulate the value of the companies' stock. It all worked great…until it didn't.

Why it Matters

Leaders who intentionally go out of their way to deceive others cannot be trusted! The moment leaders can no longer be trusted, they immediately start doing their impression of Captain Edward Smith of the RMS Titanic, because the organization is going down.

A Litmus Test

As a Forensic Leadership Pathologist, signs of deception include leaders who are inconsistent in their messaging. They tell whatever audience they are speaking to at the time exactly what that audience wants to hear. The clichés, "Just between you and me," or "Don't tell anyone else this but…." are used frequently by deceptive leaders. Pay attention to leaders who seldom put things in writing, preferring instead one-on-one private conversations because these individuals strive to create a culture in which they can continuously re-interpret events to fit their needs at the time.

When you observe an organization, whose people are not afforded an opportunity to have a clear understanding of what is transpiring within that organization, congratulations, you have observed the malignly of deception in action.

Note: deception is not a fast-acting malignancy. Because deception is often subtle in nature, the effects are slower to metastasize within the organization.

<table>
<tr><th colspan="4">Forensic Leadership Analysis ™.</th></tr>
<tr><td colspan="4">Evaluator:</td></tr>
<tr><td colspan="4">Organization:</td></tr>
<tr><td colspan="4">Leadership Autopsy Toe Tag ™</td></tr>
<tr><td colspan="4">Instructions: Check “Yes” if behavior is observable. Check “No” if the behavior is not observable. If behavior is present, circle Value. Add all circled scores together to generate a total score. Compare total score to Evaluation Scale.</td></tr>
<tr><td>Malignant Behaviors</td><td>Observed
Yes</td><td>Value</td><td>Observed
No</td></tr>
<tr><td>Deception</td><td>✓</td><td>4</td><td></td></tr>
</table>

Example:
Deception identified as “Observed” on a Leadership Autopsy Toe Tag

Malignant Leadership Characteristic #9 ***Dismissiveness***

Dismissiveness: noun

Definition:

To dismiss or reject someone or something: having or showing a disdainful attitude toward someone or something regarded as unworthy of serious attention.

Examples of dismissiveness include the following;

On July 19 - 20, 1848, Seneca Fall, New York, held one of our nation's earliest women's civil rights convention. Elizabeth Stanton, along with select female Quakers from the region, planned the two-day conference. The convention would serve as the catalyst for what later would become the suffragette movement and women's right to vote. Ultimately women in the United States would be granted the right to vote on August 26, 1920; however, in 1848, the concept of women having the right to vote was summarily dismissed.

"I know more about ISIS (the Islamic State militant group) than the Generals do. Believe

> me." November 2015, President Donald Trump
>
> "I think nobody knows more about taxes than I do, maybe in the history of the world. Nobody knows more about taxes." May 2016, President Donald Trump
>
> "Not even God himself could sink this ship." An employee of the White Star Line, at the launch of the Titanic, May 31, 1911

Why it Matters

When a leader is dismissive, the first thing it means is that they have no respect for the knowledge or abilities of the individuals who report to them. The second thing that is important to remember is that dismissive leaders are typically unteachable. Because they are not open to hearing differing perspectives, they are unable and often unwilling to learn anything more than what they currently hold to be true.

A Litmus Test

As a Forensic Leadership Pathologist, when you hear a leader say things such as, "I know more about…(whatever)….then anyone else," or "Nobody knows as much about…(whatever it is)….than I do," or you notice that the leader refuses to listen to anyone who thinks differently than they do, you have identified the malignancy of dismissiveness in action.

<table>
<tr><th colspan="4">Forensic Leadership Analysis TM.</th></tr>
<tr><td colspan="4">Evaluator:</td></tr>
<tr><td colspan="4">Organization:</td></tr>
<tr><td colspan="4">Leadership Autopsy Toe Tag TM</td></tr>
<tr><td colspan="4">Instructions: Check "Yes" if behavior is observable. Check "No" if the behavior is not observable. If behavior is present, circle Value. Add all circled scores together to generate a total score. Compare total score to Evaluation Scale.</td></tr>
<tr><td>Malignant Behaviors</td><td>Observed
Yes</td><td>Value</td><td>Observed
No</td></tr>
<tr><td>Dismissiveness</td><td>✓</td><td>4</td><td></td></tr>
</table>

Example:
Dismissiveness identified as "Observed" on a Leadership Autopsy Toe Tag

Malignant Leadership Characteristic #10 ***Manipulation***

Manipulation: noun

Definition:

The action of manipulating someone in a clever or unscrupulous way.

Examples of manipulation include the following;

Georgia cheating scandal: Eleven teachers found guilty of racketeering. "The cheating had been going on so long, we considered it part of our jobs," Jackie Parks, a former third-grade teacher at Venetian Hills elementary school and witness for the prosecution, told the New Your Times in 2013."

Martha Helen Stewart is an American retail businesswoman, writer, television personality, former model, and convicted felon. "According to the U. S. Securities and Exchange Commission (SEC), As a results of insider trading, "Stewart avoided a loss of $45,673 by selling all 3,928 shares of her ImClone Systems stock on December 27, 2001, after receiving material, nonpublic information" from her stockbroker at Merrill Lynch (Wikipedia).

George Pape, a jury foreman in a 1987 trial of John Gotti, sought out Gotti's underlings, who agreed to pay him $75,000 in exchange for a not guilty vote. Pape was later convicted of jury tampering and sentenced to three years imprisonment.

Why it Matters

When leaders introduce the malignancy of manipulation into an organization, what they are doing is bolstering an acute awareness, to every member within the organization, that the leadership will never have their backs. Manipulative leaders create a culture of fear and uncertainty. Where fear and doubt are present, trust is absent.

A Litmus Test

As a Forensic Leadership Pathologist when you observe leaders who consistently act in ways that advance only their personal needs, when you identify leaders who operate out of a win/lose mentality and believes that only they should be allow to win, you have successfully identified the malignancy of manipulation in action.

Forensic Leadership Analysis TM.			
Evaluator:			
Organization:			
Leadership Autopsy Toe Tag TM			
Instructions: Check "Yes" if behavior is observable. Check "No" if the behavior is not observable. If behavior is present, circle Value. Add all circled scores together to generate a total score. Compare total score to Evaluation Scale.			
Malignant Behaviors	Observed **Yes**	Value	Observed **No**
Manipulation	✓	4	

Example:
Manipulation identified as "Observed" on a Leadership Autopsy Toe Tag

Malignant Leadership Characteristic #11 ***Inconsistency***

Inconsistency: noun

Definition:

The quality or state of being inconsistent.

Examples of inconsistency include the following;

In the movie The Godfather, Michael Corleone, played by Al Pacino, secures his power base by doing something most unexpected. Michael talks about never making business personal, while at the same time kills the heads of all rival families to send a personal message that he is now in charge.

Walmart exhibits inconsistency in its business practices. The Walmart home page proudly states "Walmart is a place of opportunity. Here, you can go as far as your hard work and talent will take you." At the same time, Walmart is accused of gender bias. "The U.S. Equal Employment Opportunity Commission (EEOC) says that Walmart likely discriminated against 178 female workers by paying them less, denying them promotions or both, because of their gender."

(https://www.cohenmilstein.com/update/ "walmart-likely-discriminated-against-female-store-workers-eeoc-finds"-wall-street-journal)

An excellent example of inconsistency can be observed in the character of Nurse Ratchet from the movie, One Flew Over the Cuckoo's Nest. As a nurse, she is responsible for providing medical care to the individuals in her charge, yet, in her performance of her duties, she was not always caring and compassionate in the performance of her duties.

Why it Matters

When a structure is built on solid bedrock, it is built to withstand the adversity of the ages. However, when a structure is built on constantly shifting sands, it will crumble as assuredly as the movement of the shifting sands. In any organization, leadership inconsistency has the same effect as shifting sands. Inconsistent leaders do not foster a well-grounded, stable, and robust organizational culture.

A Litmus Test

Typical, malignant leaders who model inconsistently take great pride in keeping everyone off balance. Inconsistent, malignant leaders, often view the practice of consistency as an inherent leadership weakness; they value erratic behavior because it allows them to be in total control at all times.

As a Forensic Leadership Pathologist, pay attention to a leader's organizational priorities. If you observe that their priorities are constantly shifting, that their behavior is erratic, that there is a lack of long-term vision and commitment, and no clearly articulated strategic vision for the future, congratulations, you have identified the malignancy of inconsistency in practice.

Forensic Leadership Analysis ™.			
Evaluator:			
Organization:			
Leadership Autopsy Toe Tag ™			
Instructions: Check "Yes" if behavior is observable. Check "No" if the behavior is not observable. If behavior is present, circle Value. Add all circled scores together to generate a total score. Compare total score to Evaluation Scale.			
Malignant Behaviors	Observed **Yes**	Value	Observed **No**
Inconsistency	✓	3	

Example:

Inconsistency identified as "Observed" on a Leadership Autopsy Toe Tag

Malignant Leadership Characteristic #12 ***Unteachable***

Unteachability: noun

Definition:

Unable to be taught: not teachable.

Examples of unteachable include the following;

Alford Lord Tennyson is his famous poem The Charge of the Light Brigade provides us with an excellent literary example of exactly what happens when a leader is unable, or unwilling, to learn and adapt. 40% of the soldiers involved in the fateful Calvary charge were either killed or wounded. In today's business world, there is no glory for those who blindly follow, only an unemployment line.

An estimated 23,000,000 military personal were killed or wounded in WWI. Many of these service members, on both sides, were unfortunate victims of leadership that was unable, or unwilling to adapt their strategies to the new technologies they were facing. The military leaders of the day, who were unable to learn from their previous failures, kept insisting that "going over the top" in massive frontal assaults was the only way for their men to fight the war.

While Rush Limbaugh may not be a leader, he does provide us with an excellent example of what being unteachable looks like in practice. Limbaugh has made a living as a conservative talk show host. His shtick is to take a stance on a particular topic, and no matter what, never change his mind. He is not able to accept any new data or facts that differ from what he believes to be true. Rush Limbaugh is the poster boy for what unteachable looks like in action.

Why it Matters

Unteachable leaders often mistakenly believe that they know it all. They portray a sense of entitlement, believing that the rules do not apply to them. They have little to no tolerance for failure or people who fail them. Unteachable leaders often think they are better off doing everything themselves because no one else is as smart or capable as they are.

A Litmus Test

As a Forensic Leadership Pathologist, it is easy to spot unteachable leaders because they are seldom either willing or able to modify their originally held position or belief—even when new evidence, or data, suggests it would be wise to do so. Unteachable leaders keep making the same mistakes over, and over, and over, and over.

As a Forensic Leadership Pathologist, when you observe leaders with established track records of failure, who refuse to learn from their mistakes and are unwilling to listen to advice from others far more knowledgeable about the subject, you have identified the malignancy of unteachability in action.

Forensic Leadership Analysis TM.			
Evaluator:			
Organization:			
Leadership Autopsy Toe Tag TM			
Instructions: Check "Yes" if behavior is observable. Check "No" if the behavior is not observable. If behavior is present, circle Value. Add all circled scores together to generate a total score. Compare total score to Evaluation Scale.			
Malignant Behaviors	Observed **Yes**	Value	Observed **No**
Unteachability	✓	3	

Example:
Unteachability identified as "Observed" on a Leadership Autopsy Toe Tag

Malignant Leadership Characteristic #13

Gamesmanship

Gamesmanship: noun

Definition:

The art of winning games by using various ploys and tactics to gain a psychological advantage.

Examples of gamesmanship include the following;

Winner of seven Academy Awards in 1973, including Best Picture, The Sting, starring Paul Newman and Robert Redford, represents the epitome of gamesmanship at multiple levels. The takeaway from this picture is, when people play games, nothing is what it seems.

Ocean's Eleven starring George Clooney, Brad Pitt, and Matt Damon is a modern twist at gamesmanship in action. This film does an excellent job of depicting the misdirection and misunderstanding that comes to fruition when individuals allow gamesmanship to govern their decision-making processes.

> Kim Jong-un, the Leader of North Korea, employed the technique of saber-rattling when he promised a "Christmas gift" for the Americans in 2019. Saber-rattling is a very popular form of gamesmanship between opposing countries.

Why it Matters

The responsibility for leading others is never a game. It is one of, if not the only, most serious endeavor and responsibility an individual can ever undertake. Any leaders who think of it as a game do not deserve, nor should they every be afforded, a position of leadership because they are not fit to be leaders.

A Litmus Test

As a Forensic Leadership Pathologist, look for leaders who arbitrarily move the performance goal post, arbitrarily change the rules and accountability measures, intentionally send different messages to different members of the team, encourage internal conflicts and political battles, or encourage competing agendas within the organization. When you see these behaviors in practice, you have identified the malignancy of gamesmanship in action.

Forensic Leadership Analysis ™.			
Evaluator:			
Organization:			
Leadership Autopsy Toe Tag ™			
Instructions: Check "Yes" if behavior is observable. Check "No" if the behavior is not observable. If behavior is present, circle Value. Add all circled scores together to generate a total score. Compare total score to Evaluation Scale.			
Malignant Behaviors	Observed **Yes**	Value	Observed **No**
Gamesmanship	✓	3	

Example:
Gamesmanship identified as "Observed" on a Leadership Autopsy Toe Tag

Collectively, these thirteen (13) characteristics comprise the Forensic Leadership Autopsy Toe Tag show in its entirety below.

Forensic Leadership Analysis TM.			
Evaluator:			
Organization:			
Leadership Autopsy Toe Tag TM			
Instructions: Check "Yes" if behavior is observable. Check "No" if the behavior is not observable. If behavior is present, circle Value. Add all circled scores together to generate a total score. Compare total score to Evaluation Scale.			
Malignant Behaviors	Observed **Yes**	Value	Observed **No**
Lying		6	
Hubris		6	
Avarice		6	
Duplicity		6	
Cunning		5	
Narcissism		5	
Disconnection		5	
Deception		4	
Dismissiveness		4	
Manipulation		4	
Inconsistency		3	
Unteachability		3	
Gamesmanship		3	
	Total Score		
Evaluation Scale	**Levels**		**Action**
Score 40 - 60	Dying Organization		**Run!**
Score 21 - 39	Malignancy Spreading		**Update Resume**
Score 1 - 20	Malignancy Present		**Observe Closely**

Use the 13 malignant characteristics listed on the Leadership Toe Tag to guide your observations when performing a Leadership Autopsy. Identify each of the malignant leadership characteristics you observe that are present in the organizational culture. Total the values to generate a cumulative score and take the appropriate action.

There are two very important things to understand about malignant leadership. First, malignant leadership will destroy an organization. It not a question of if, it's a question of when. Second, malignant leaders have a tendency to introduce more than one malignant behavior into an organization. You will find in most dysfunctional organizations, several, and in some cases all, of the malignant behaviors listed on the Toe Tag.

The process of performing a Leadership Autopsy starts by honing one's ability to observe. Observe how leaders conduct themselves in public, observe a leader's actual business practices. Observe an organization's leadership in action when they don't think anyone is looking. Observe how leaders treat their employees at all levels throughout the organization. Observe how a company treats its customers. When it comes to identifying an organization's real culture, actions always speak louder than words, which is why we learn to ignore the rhetoric and focus purely on the actions. Organizational culture is what you see happening in front of you, your observations, and your observations alone, are the only things that matter.

It is time to put your knowledge as a Forensic Leadership Pathologist to work. We will start by using the Leadership Autopsy Toe Tag to analyze several real-world case studies. These case studies are for instructional purposes only.

E.F. Hutton

Malignant Leadership Case Study #1

"When E. F. Hutton talks, people listen."

The Facts

In 1988, the brokerage firm of E. F. Hutton was not only well respected within the financial sector, it was considered by many to be the industry leader, so well established that "When E. F. Hutton speaks, people listen." Then suddenly, it all went wrong, and the company that had been the stocks and bonds Rock of Gibraltar simply crumbled. A critical examination of the decisions and behavior of the E.F. Hutton leadership at that time affords us the ability to understand how and why a company that seemed to have it all, ended up with nothing.

E. F. Hutton was first formed in 1904. From its humble beginning in a single room in New York's financial district Hutton, at its height, would employ 19,000 employees, along with 6,500 account executives, and operate in 383 domestic and 18 foreign branch offices serving roughly 1.7 million clients. Edward Hutton, the founder, led the firm until his death in 1962. By the early 1980s, the brokerage house he founded had become the principal component of what grew into a conglomerate of companies owned by E. F. Hutton Group Inc., listed on the New York Stock Exchange. Other subsidiaries of that Delaware-charter holding company were E. F. Hutton Trust Company (now "Smith Barney Corporate Trust Company" and owned by Citigroup), E. F. Hutton Life Insurance Company, and E. F. Hutton Bank. The Hutton companies also managed many mutual funds and other investment vehicles, some of which were separately incorporated and/or registered and participated actively in corporate mergers and public offerings of securities.

The beginning of the end of E.F. Hutton would start under the watchful eye of Robert M. Fomon, Chairman and Chief Executive Officer of E. F. Hutton from 1970 to 1987, a short 12 years after the passing of its founder.

New Leadership Decisions

On an afternoon in May of 1978, the new money mobilizer for E.F. Hutton & Co. explained an aggressive new cash management system to executives from the brokerage's nine regional offices who had gathered in a

Kansas City hotel. Using a blackboard and charts, William Sullivan Jr. showed his colleagues how they could use his new system for regularly over-drafting company bank accounts to extract substantial profits in interest income for Hutton. In 1980, several Hutton branches actively began writing checks greater than what they had on hand at one bank, then making a deposit in another bank equal to the amount it wrote at the first bank. This strategy, known as "chaining", is a form of check kiting. "Chaining" gave Hutton the use of money in both accounts until the checks cleared. In effect, Hutton was giving itself a free loan that also did not carry any interest. Several executives openly and eagerly embraced this new accounting miracle, eagerly supported and promoted the new overdraft practice to their branch managers across the country. The profits generated through this accounting sleight of hand would ultimately be the undoing of E. F. Hutton because the branch managers, who's bonuses were based on the profits generated from this practice, maximized use of the practice to realize the largest bonuses possible.

The Smoking Gun

"Thomas Morley, who was in charge of getting the firm to manage its cash better, wrote a memo to Hutton's president, George Ball, saying that this practice netted one branch an extra $30,000 per month. Ball sent the memo out across Hutton's network of regional sales managers, with the note, "A point well-remembered, and acted on."

Over the years, Hutton shuffled money in this manner between 400 banks (mostly small rural banks), gaining the use of an estimated $250 million a day without paying a penny in interest.

The scheme worked for almost three years until officials at the Genesee County Bank in Batavia, New York, discovered that the large deposits made by Hutton's four-person office there were far more than the office's banking requirements. They also discovered that the checks Hutton was using to make the deposits were drawn on two Pennsylvania banks.

When Genesee officials learned that Hutton did not have enough money in the Pennsylvania bank accounts to cover the checks, they stopped honoring Hutton checks. One of the banks involved, United Penn Bank (now part of Citizens Financial Group), asked the Federal Deposit Insurance Corporation to investigate. In 1984, the matter was forwarded to the United States Attorney for the Middle District of Pennsylvania, who opened a federal criminal probe.

Of particular interest, it should be noted that whenever one of the smaller regional banks sensed something was amiss, Hutton's leadership bullied those banks into submission by questioning the smaller bank's procedures.

When it finally realized it was in trouble, E. F. Hutton retained Tom Curnin, a respected defense attorney who was inclined to fight the government. However, in February 1985, Curnin discovered a memo from a Hutton regional vice-president for the Washington D. C., area which stated that his offices drew on "bogus deposits." The memo was tantamount to an admission of guilt and led Curnin to abandon his tradition of deny and fight it tactics, instead Curnin recommended that Hutton negotiate for a plea agreement.

In the spring of 1985, Curnin told Hutton's board that it faced two choices: plead guilty to a massive list of felonies or face a trial that would likely see three senior Hutton executives convicted and drive Hutton out of business. Curnin advised settling with the government to avoid years of bad publicity. As a part of the plea deal, Curnin was able to negate the following two major concessions.

First, no Hutton executives would be prosecuted, even though the government would ultimately determine that twenty-five senior officers colluded to masterminded this check kiting scheme.

Second, the Securities and Exchange Commission allowed Hutton to stay in business; offenses of this magnitude usually result in an individual or firm being permanently barred from the securities industry.

An internal review conducted by former Attorney General Griffin Bell concluded that the scam occurred due to inadequate internal controls.

The report absolved top Hutton executives of direct responsibility for criminal actions. Bell said neither Robert Fomon, the chairman and chief executive officer of Hutton, nor former president George Ball, then head of Prudential-Bache Securities, was responsible for failing to detect the abuses. But Bell chastised Hutton`s corporate structure for failure to install auditing systems that should have uncovered or prevented the scheme.

As if to add an exclamation mark to the rampant internal corruption and culture of deceit, in early 1987, an internal E. F. Hutton probe revealed that brokers at an office in Providence, Rhode Island, had knowingly laundered money for the Patriarca crime family who operated businesses throughout New England.

Consequences

On May 2, Hutton agreed to plead guilty to 2,000 counts of mail fraud, as well as pay a $2 million fine plus $750,000 for the cost of the investigation. Hutton also agreed to pay $8 million in restitution, the estimated extra income earned from the fraud.

By the end of November, Hutton had lost $76 million, mainly due to massive trading losses and margin calls that its customers could not meet. It also had its commercial rating cut from A-2 to A-3, effectively losing $1.3 million in financing. Hutton was now weeks, perhaps days, according to some board members from collapse.

Due to its massive financial losses, E. F. Hutton was put on sale as early as 1986, but would not find a buyer for two years. E. F. Hutton would finally merge with Shearson Lehman American Express on December 3, 1988, for the bargain sale price of approximately $1 billion.

A Final Irony

By the end of 1986, the E. F. Hutton brand had been severely damaged and almost completely destroyed. In response, a $20 million marketing campaign was launched with the specific intent of rebuilding the brand. E. F. Hutton would pay a spokesman they deemed “highly credible” $3 million to make approximately ten commercials; that spokesman was none other than Mr. Bill Cosby.

When it was all over, the damage done to E.F. Hutton by its leadership was so devastating that when E.F. Hutton spoke, no one cared.

Forensic Leadership Analysis TM.			
Evaluator:			
Organization:			
Leadership Autopsy Toe Tag TM			
Instructions: Check "Yes" if behavior is observable. Check "No" if the behavior is not observable. If behavior is present, circle Value. Add all circled scores together to generate a total score. Compare total score to Evaluation Scale.			
Malignant Behaviors	Observed **Yes**	Value	Observed **No**
Lying		6	
Hubris		6	
Avarice		6	
Duplicity		6	
Cunning		5	
Narcissism		5	
Disconnection		5	
Deception		4	
Dismissiveness		4	
Manipulation		4	
Inconsistency		3	
Unteachability		3	
Gamesmanship		3	
	Total Score		
Evaluation Scale	**Levels**		**Action**
Score 40 - 60	Dying Organization		**Run!**
Score 21 - 39	Malignancy Spreading		**Update Resume**
Score 1 - 20	Malignancy Present		**Observe Closely**

Schlitz Brewery

Malignant Leadership Case Study #2

> "A classic tale of human failing, the Schlitz saga now serves as a reminder for those who might lose sight of the fact that a company – no matter how modern its plants, how endowed its balance sheet, or how lionized by Wall Street analysts, is really no stronger than the human beings who manage it."
>
> *Carl Swanson*

The story of Schlitz brewery, and the beer that made Milwaukee famous, serves as a pleasant reminder that given the wrong leadership, and enough time, just about anything is possible.

The Facts

Between 1900 and 1950, Schlitz brewery and Anheuser-Busch were running neck & neck (that's a beer bottle joke), often taking turns as the #1 brewer in the nation. Then the wheels came off when the Schlitz leadership couldn't stand the heat in the brewhouse.

The Schlitz brewing company initially began in 1849 when a German immigrant by the name of August

Krug started brewing beer in his basement. August Krug would hire Joseph Schlitz as a bookkeeper. Through a series of events, two years later, Krug would die, and Joseph Schlitz would take over the business, renaming it Schlitz Brewery. At that same time, Joseph Schlitz would hire August Uihlein, the sixteen-year-old nephew of August Krug, who would ultimately take over the company when Joseph Schlitz died in 1875 in a shipwreck while on vacation in Europe.

August Uihlein had a simple vision, "Make a great tasting beer!". August Uihlein hired his three brothers to help him expand the brewery. For nearly 60 years, the Uihlein brothers would scour the world, purchasing only the finest ingredients necessary to make a great tasting beer.

The desire to make great beer would all come to a head in 1967 when Robert Uihlein Jr., took the helm. Robert Uihlein Jr. was a Harvard graduate. As a businessman he possessed a better understanding of balance sheets than he did the brewing process. Even though he attended the U.S. Brewers Academy, Robert Uihlein Jr. failed as a leader and Brewmaster. Unlike his predecessors, August Krug, Joseph Schlitz, and August Uihlein, Robert Uihlein Jr. had no interest in making great beer; he simply wanted to make as much money as possible and saw beer as the vehicle to do so.

In the early 1970s, Schlitz CEO Robert Uihlein, Jr., was faced with the interesting challenge of trying to increase market share at a time when Anheuser-Busch was dominating the marketplace.

Robert Uihlein Jr. developed a bold strategy to compete against Anheuser-Busch. He reasoned that if Schlitz could cut the cost of the ingredients they used in making beer, and, if they could speed up the brewing process, they could make a cheaper beer, in a shorter time. The end result would mean higher profits. It was brilliant!

Because Robert Uihlein Jr. knew enough about brewing to be dangerous, but not enough about brewing to make great tasting beer, he decided to make a few necessary changes to the recipe.

- He instructed his brewers to replace some of the malted barley with corn syrup.
- He instructed his brewers to start using much cheaper hop pellets instead of the fresh hops they had traditionally used.
- The corn syrup made the beer murky, requiring the addition of silica gel to the beer to control the hazing effect it developed the bottle.

- Fearing that they would have to list the ingredients of the silica gel on the label, Schlitz was forced to quit using the gel and began using a different haze agent called Chill-garde, which caused the beer to form white protein flakes, which as they fell to the bottom of the bottle coagulated into the consistency of snot.

Robert Uihlein Jr. had mastered the art of making cheap, snotty, horribly tasting beer quickly. While the beer may have been horrendous, the profits were anything but. Robert Uihlein Jr. had found the recipe for making money. With these new brewing techniques now refined, Robert Uihlein Jr. could focus on doing what he did best.

When consumers started to complain about the texture of the beer, Uihlein first ignored their concerns, then denied the problem existed. Finally, some six months later Robert Uihlein Jr. explained that while the beer may look like sludge, with a bonus snot factor at the bottom of every bottle, "the haze was not actually physically harmful to drinkers." After six months of consumer complaints, Schlitz recalled 10 million cans of snot beer.

Still, Robert Uihlein Jr. was not familiar with the old adage, when you're in a hole, the first thing you need to do is stop digging. So, he grabbed a shovel and got busy.

- Schlitz launched a new “high impact" add campaign featuring a boxer who was being asked to give up Schlitz. The ad campaign bombed with consumers “who found it menacing, and it became known as the "Drink Schlitz or I'll kill you!" campaign.”
- Robert Uihlein Jr. decided to mislead the public by redefining the acronym ABF from “accelerated batch fermentation” to “accurate balance fermentation” as a way to explain and justify their reduced brew time. Schlitz could manufacture a batch of beer in 15 days while a better batch of beer would take their competitor Anheuser-Busch 40 days to brew.
- In 1981 Schlitz leadership had Union problems. Schlitz leadership had distanced themselves from their workforce and were holding strong for a no pay increase for all Milwaukee union workers.
- As a cost-saving for the company, Schlitz fired all company beer drivers and outsourced the

distribution process to local beverage distributors.

- Robert Uihlein Jr., the Harvard graduate, watched as Schlitz stock went from $65 to $5 per share.

Given all of the above, still, it wasn't until "June 1, 1981, when more than 700 members of Brewery Workers Local 9 walked off their jobs," that the beginning of the end came into focus. Two months later, with picket lines still in place, Schlitz announced it would end brewing operations in Milwaukee.

Schlitz would ultimately go out of business, proving that failed leadership can and will destroy even the healthiest and most profitable of organizations.

Forensic Leadership Analysis TM.			
Evaluator:			
Organization:			
Leadership Autopsy Toe Tag TM			
Instructions: Check "Yes" if behavior is observable. Check "No" if the behavior is not observable. If behavior is present, circle Value. Add all circled scores together to generate a total score. Compare total score to Evaluation Scale.			
Malignant Behaviors	Observed **Yes**	Value	Observed **No**
Lying		6	
Hubris		6	
Avarice		6	
Duplicity		6	
Cunning		5	
Narcissism		5	
Disconnection		5	
Deception		4	
Dismissiveness		4	
Manipulation		4	
Inconsistency		3	
Unteachability		3	
Gamesmanship		3	
	Total Score		

Evaluation Scale	**Levels**	**Action**
Score 40 - 60	Dying Organization	**Run!**
Score 21 - 39	Malignancy Spreading	**Update Resume**
Score 1 - 20	Malignancy Present	**Observe Closely**

Chase National Bank

Malignant Leadership Case Study #3

"It is doubtful if there was another instance of a corporate executive who so thoroughly and successfully used his official and fiduciary position for private profit"

US Senate Banking Committee member
Ferdinand Pecora

The Facts

Albert Henry Wiggins was born in 1868 and lived until 1951. He started working in the financial sector in 1894. Working for Chase National Bank, he proved to be an innovator in the area of finance, enough so that in 1904 he was promoted to Vice-President, the youngest Vice-President in the history of the institution. His meteoric rise to even greater positions of authority continued until finally, in 1911, upon the retirement of then President Henry W. Cannon, Wiggins was named President of Chase National Bank. During this same time, Wiggins also served as a representative on 50 other financial institutions boards. (How he found time to actually work is a mystery.)

As the President, he significantly grew the financial resources of the institution orchestrating seven bank mergers—a first for the industry at the time - which grew bank deposits from $91 million dollars in 1910 to $2.7 billion dollars by the end of 1917. In addition, Wiggins was quite effective in growing the number of shareholders. He increased the number of shareholders from twenty in 1904, to 2,189 in 1921, 50,510 in 1929, and finally 89,000 by 1933. The increase in the number of shareholders not only added hundreds of millions of dollars to the company profits, it also caught the attention of John Rockefeller, who decided to shift some of his vast financial resources into the Chase National Bank. By all accounts, Chase National Bank appeared to be in good hands right up until the great stock market crash of 1929.

The Great Depression would run from 1929 until 1939. The crash was a result of erratic and irrational behaviors on the part of Wall Street Investors who panicked. One man who did not panic was Albert Wiggins, along with some of his closest associates who quickly realized for those few individuals who possess the courage, insider trading knowledge, and the ability to foster financial collusion, among the winds of chaos also blow the winds of opportunity.

Insider Trading

The surest legitimate way to make money over time in the stock market is to buy low and sell high. However, the most efficient way to reap the greatest amount of profit in the stock market, with the smallest amount of risk, is to be on the right side of insider trading.

Insider trading is illegal! Insider trading occurs when an individual buys or sells stocks they have in a company using information that is not available to the general public.

Hypothetically, suppose I was the CEO of a new start-up tech company located in American Falls, Idaho, called FixIT. FixIT specializes in GPS navigational software development.

Let's suppose I have a six-member Board of Directors, all extremely wealthy individuals who reside in various locations throughout Idaho. Known only to me at the time, JetPAC recently notified me that FixIT would soon be awarded a five-billion-dollar, two-year contract, to develop the GPS software for the rocket JetPAC intends to send to Mars. Excited about the news, I call my Board to tell them the good news, FixIT has hit it big! Understanding the financial implications this five-billion-dollar contract will have on the stock value of the company, Board members take out their checkbooks and quickly purchase five-million additional shares each of FixIT stock at the current price of $5 a share.

Two weeks later, JetPAC announces publicly that they have awarded FixIT a five-billion dollar contract to develop the guidance system for the Mars rocket. Public interest in FixIT goes through the roof. As a result of the announcement, demand for FixIT stock skyrockets! Over the next week, FixIT sells 50,000,000 new shares of stock, and the value of the stock rises from $5 to $89 a share. My Board members are ecstatic. Their initial $25,000,000 investment has resulted in a net profit to each of them of $395,000,000. Everyone is happy because they were able to make the most amount of profit with the least amount of risk. Everybody loves a sure thing, and nothing is as surely reliable as insider trading.

This is essentially what Albert Wiggins did with his 42,000 shares of Chase National Bank stock. In the Stock Market crash of 1929, investors panicked and started selling stocks; over sixteen million shares were sold on the exchange on Black Tuesday alone. In 1929, sixteen million shares were the largest number of stocks ever traded on the exchange in a single day. Declining stock prices were wiping out personal wealth quickly, and no one understood this better than the President of Chase National Bank, Albert Wiggins, as he watched the values of his Chase National Bank shares plummet in value.

Wiggins had a plan. Because Wiggins served on over 50 boards, his connections afforded him the ability to convince other influential bankers to pool their money to create a massive financial investment pool. At a time when everyone else was selling, these bankers single-handedly attempted to stop the market from further collapse.

On Black Tuesday, the bankers looking for their biggest bang for their bucks, sent Richard Whitney, the vice-president of the New York Stock Exchange, onto the floor of the exchange, with all the bravado of Donald Trump announcing another win. His goal was to purchase a number of select stocks with as much fanfare as possible, as a sign of their faith in the market. Whitley started the day by buying select stocks *above* market value. Fortunately for Albert Wiggins, Chase National Bank just happened to be one of those stocks the investment pool was purchasing. Chase National Bank President Albert Wiggins, and several his closest friends, who also just happened to be selling their shares of Chase

National Bank stocks were reaping a whirlwind of profits.

As Steve Jobs is famous for saying, "But wait, there's more." Realizing that while what he was doing was not illegal (insider trading was not illegal in 1929), Wiggins was aware that if his actions were discovered, they could possibly damage his public image. At that time in history, the president of a bank could not afford to have a public image problem. Always one step ahead of everyone else, Wiggins made sure to conduct the sales of his 42,0000 shares under his wife's name and through a shell company he had created. Now for the masterstroke of innovation. Wiggins made sure his shell company was located in Canada; thus, Wiggins also avoided paying any income tax on the $4,000,000 he made selling his Chase National Bank stock. In 1929 $4,000,000 was a lot of money!

Congress Was Appalled

In 1932, as a direct result of the egregious behavior on the part of Albert Henry Wiggins, the United States Congress passed the Exchange Act. The Exchange Act officially made insider trading by corporate executives illegal. In 1932, the banking leadership in American was so broken; it took an act of Congress forcing bankers to act ethically. Obviously, when it comes to the financial sector in the United States, "the more things change, the more things stay the same."

Forensic Leadership Analysis TM.			
Evaluator:			
Organization:			
Leadership Autopsy Toe Tag TM			
Instructions: Check "Yes" if behavior is observable. Check "No" if the behavior is not observable. If behavior is present, circle Value. Add all circled scores together to generate a total score. Compare total score to Evaluation Scale.			
Malignant Behaviors	Observed **Yes**	Value	Observed **No**
Lying		6	
Hubris		6	
Avarice		6	
Duplicity		6	
Cunning		5	
Narcissism		5	
Disconnection		5	
Deception		4	
Dismissiveness		4	
Manipulation		4	
Inconsistency		3	
Unteachability		3	
Gamesmanship		3	
	Total Score		
Evaluation Scale	**Levels**		**Action**
Score 40 - 60	Dying Organization		**Run!**
Score 21 - 39	Malignancy Spreading		**Update Resume**
Score 1 - 20	Malignancy Present		**Observe Closely**

Baylor University

Malignant Leadership Case Study #4

"Baylor University has resisted all efforts to provide the public with information which would reveal the conduct of the senior administration, and instead attempted to put the blame entirely on football coaches."

Texas State Representative Roland Gutierrez

Just the Facts

Baylor University, founded in 1845, is a private Baptist university located in Waco, Texas. Baylor, a member institution of the Big 12 Conference, serves approximately 16,000 students annually. It is recognized for the George W. Truett Theological Seminary and the Baylor Law School, the oldest law school in Texas. Baylor University is currently accredited by the Southern Association of Colleges and Schools.

From 2012 - 2016, an emerging national dominant football team was responsible for bringing a flood of national recognition to the university. Unfortunately, it was not the kind of recognition the university wanted. At the heart of the problem are two prominent figures, Baylor University President, Kenneth Winston Starr (President 2010 - 2016), and Head Football Coach Art Briles (Head Football Coach 2007 - 2016). Briles led the 2011 Baylor team in its most successful season since the formation of the Big 12 Conference in 1996. With Baylor's win in the 2011 Valero Alamo Bowl game, Briles led the Bears to a 10–3 record. The only other time Baylor has won as many as ten games was in 1980. As good as the football team was performing on the field, off-the-field behavior left something to be desired. President Starr is reported as saying as the football program rose in national prominence, "standards fell overboard."

The first sign of trouble occurred in 2015 when former players Sam Ukwuachu and Tevin Elliot were accused of sexual assault. However, these allegations were simply the tip of the iceberg. "John Clune, a Colorado lawyer who specializes in cases of campus assault and who had already resolved three other women's claims against Baylor, filed a lawsuit on behalf of an alleged victim that sought, in part, to quantify the crisis at Baylor. Clune's lawsuit "made the startling claim that at least 52 rapes by at least 31 players had occurred from 2011 through 2014, a period when the once-hapless Baylor football program became a dominant force in the highly competitive Big 12 Conference" (College Football 2017).

As allegations surrounding a football culture at Baylor University became an all too common occurrence, Baylor University turned to the courts for protection.

"A federal judge rejected Baylor's request to throw out a lawsuit filed against the university by 10 women who say they were sexually assaulted while they were students. Judge Robert L. Pitman of Federal District Court ruled that each plaintiff had "plausibly alleged that Baylor was deliberately indifferent to her report(s) of sexual assault, depriving her of educational opportunities to which she was entitled."

The Baylor culture was a complex problem that did not manifest itself overnight. There were a lot of moving parts within the organization, each adding to the complexity of the situation.

Emmitt Knowlton provides an excellent overview of the problem inherent to Baylor in his article entitled "Damning Report Reveals Horrifying Extent of Baylor Sexual-assault Scandal that Led to Football Coach's Ouster," published by Business Insider 2016. (http://www.businessinsider.com/baylor-sexual-assault-scandal-report-art-briles-2016-5).

Knowlton reports, "…the university released the findings of an independent investigation conducted by the law firm Pepper Hamilton, which the school had hired in fall 2015 to investigate its handling of accusations of sexual assault. The findings, which can be read in full on Baylor's website, (https://www.baylor.edu/thefacts/doc.php/266596.pdf) paint a damning picture of culture that failed to hold the football team accountable, discouraged victims from filing complaints, and, on numerous occasions, neglected to remove victims from potentially dangerous situations with assailants.

The findings:

- "The University's student conduct processes were wholly inadequate to consistently provide a prompt and equitable response under Title IX; Baylor failed to consistently support complaints through the provision of interim measures; and in some cases, the University failed to take action to identify and eliminate a potentially hostile environment, prevent its recurrence or address its effects."

- "Actions by University administrators directly discouraged some complainants from reporting or participating in student conduct processes and, in one instance, constituted retaliation against a complainant for reporting sexual assault."

- "In addition to broader University failings, Pepper found specific failings within both the football program and Athletics department leadership, including a failure to identify and respond to a pattern of sexual violence by a football player and to a report of dating violence."

- "There are significant concerns about the tone and culture within Baylor's football program as it relates to accountability for all forms of student-athlete misconduct."

- "Over the course of their review, Pepper investigated the University's response to reports of a sexual assault involving multiple football players. The football program and Athletics department leadership failed to take appropriate action in response to these reports."

Richard Willis, chair of the Baylor Board of Regents, was quoted as saying, "We were horrified by the extent of these acts of sexual violence on our campus. This investigation revealed the University's mishandling of reports in what should have been a supportive, responsive, and caring environment for students."

The Other Shoe

Baylor University's handling of this situation was rather unique. While colleges and universities are required by law to report and investigate reports of sexual assault to the appropriate authorities, Outside the Lines reported in 2016 that it took Baylor "almost two years to look at the claims against two former football players." Neither a sense of urgency or transparency are readily observable in their handling of the situation.

Further, Pepper Hamilton, the law firm hired to investigate the allegation, chose to share the results of their investigation in an oral report to the Board. The lawyers' report, however, "was delivered in the form of an oral presentation that fully and comprehensively presented the individual and aggregated findings and the evidence supporting the findings," said David Garland, interim president.

Unfortunately, as Marc Tracy also noted, "a written report of an investigation conducted by an outside law firm in the wake of several sexual assault allegations and convictions involving Baylor football players does not exist."

Former director of women's athletics at the University of Texas, Donna Lopiano, provides insight as to why Baylor failed to establish a paper trail of the investigation. "It's very common, if you don't want something discovered in court, you do not want to have a written record," Ms. Lopiano said, noting that the University of Minnesota had similarly released an eight-page "interim report" of a Title IX investigation last year after an outside lawyer's presentation was delivered orally."

Forensic Leadership Analysis TM.			
Evaluator:			
Organization:			
Leadership Autopsy Toe Tag TM			
Instructions: Check "Yes" if behavior is observable. Check "No" if the behavior is not observable. If behavior is present, circle Value. Add all circled scores together to generate a total score. Compare total score to Evaluation Scale.			
Malignant Behaviors	Observed **Yes**	Value	Observed **No**
Lying		6	
Hubris		6	
Avarice		6	
Duplicity		6	
Cunning		5	
Narcissism		5	
Disconnection		5	
Deception		4	
Dismissiveness		4	
Manipulation		4	
Inconsistency		3	
Unteachability		3	
Gamesmanship		3	
	Total Score		
Evaluation Scale	**Levels**		**Action**
Score 40 - 60	Dying Organization		**Run!**
Score 21 - 39	Malignancy Spreading		**Update Resume**
Score 1 - 20	Malignancy Present		**Observe Closely**

Penn State University

Malignant Leadership Case Study #5

"Penn State football coach Joe Paterno dismissed a sexual assault complaint made against assistant coach Jerry Sandusky by a 14-year-old boy in 1976 and the school was made aware of other allegations long before Sandusky was arrested in 2011, according to documents unsealed Tuesday in a Philadelphia courthouse."

A. J. Perez, USA Today Sports

Just the Facts

The Jerry Sandusky and Penn State sexual abuse scandal became public in November 2011. We would go on to learn that Jerry Sandusky, a former assistant football coach at Penn State for 30 years (1969 to 1999) was convicted on multiple counts of child molestation. Sandusky was charged with alleged child abuse that ranged from 1994 to 2009, although the abuse may have taken place over four decades.

Sandusky trial began on June 11, 2012 and concluded on June 22, 2014. He was convicted on 45 counts of sexual abuse and is currently serving between 30 and 60 years in prison. Even though Jerry Sandusky was found guilty on 45 counts of child abuse, it is important to note that he still maintains his innocence.

Let me start by saying the children that were harmed are always, and will always be, the most important element of this entire tragedy. They are, and will always be, what matters most. Of secondary importance to the safety and health of these victims is an understanding of the complete lapse in ethical leadership surrounding these horrific events. With that in mind, the focus of this case study will remain on the behavior of the leadership who allowed it to happen.

In 2011 Dr. Graham Spanier was the President of Penn State University. Based on the decisions he made when the Sandusky problem was brought to his attention President Spanier would later be charged with perjury, obstruction of justice, and failure to report suspected child abuse. Dr. Spanier resigned his position shortly after news of the scandal went public.

Two other university leaders involved in the Sandusky scandal included Athletic Director Timothy Curley and University Senior Vice-President for Finance and Business Gary Schultz. Ultimately, both Mr. Curley and Mr. Schultz were "found to be not credible" by the grand jury. The two administrators were charged by the grand jury with perjury and failure to report suspected child abuse. The indictment accused both Curley and Schultz of not only failing to tell the police but falsely telling the grand jury that Mike McQueary never informed them of sexual activity."

The Penn State board of trustees wanted some answers. They contracted with Freeh Sporkin & Sullivan, LLP., to find out what was going on. It turned out that Spanier, Schultz, Curley, and Paterno came up short when they were most needed. On June 30, 2012, Jo Becker of the New York Times reported the following, "E-Mails suggest Paterno role in Silence on Sandusky." Becker states, "Louis J. Freeh, the former F.B.I. Director leading an independent investigation ordered by the universities Board of Trustees suggests that the question of what to do about McQueary's report was extensively debated by university officials. These officials, the e-mail shows, included the University President Graham B. Spanier, the Athletic Director Tim Curley, the official in charge of the campus police, Senior Vice President for Finance and Business Gary Schultz, and Joe Paterno. The Penn State emails, according to the person with knowledge of the French investigation, indicated that Spanier, Curley, and Schultz seemed at one point to favor reporting the assault to the state child welfare authorities, recognized that if they did not, they could later be vulnerable to charges that they failed to act. But in one email, Curley wrote that after talking to Paterno, he no longer wanted to go forward with the plan."

Jeremy Hartley, in his article entitled McQueary Trial Continues with Testimony from Former PSU Spokesman, for centredaily.com noted that Dr. Spanier would issue a statement of support that said both Curley and Schultz had his unconditional support. He believed these men "operate at the highest levels of honesty, integrity, and compassion." President Spanier's letter goes on to say, "I am confident the record will show that these charges are groundless and that they conducted themselves professionally and appropriately." (https://www.centredaily.com/news/local/education/penn-state/jerry-sandusky/article109056707.html)

When it was all said and done, the President of the University Graham Spanier, the University Senior Vice President for Finance and Business Gary Schultz, the Athletic Director Timothy Curley, along with Head Coach Joe Paterno, decided, as four of the most influential leaders in the University at the time, that the best way to handle the situation was to remain quiet about it. As a group, they were not consistent in their execution of the "stay quiet plan" because later, Curley and Schultz would choose to lie to the grand jury. Their actions were merely reflective of the culture fostered by the leadership of the University.

- On March 13, 2017 - Curley and Schultz plead guilty to a misdemeanor charge of endangering the welfare of children in exchange for the dismissal of felony charges.
- April 30, 2019 – U.S. Magistrate Judge Karoline Mehalchick vacates Spanier's 2017 conviction for endangering the welfare of a child. Spanier was set to be sentenced on the one count conviction, instead, the court ordered the conviction be vacated because it was based on a criminal statute that did not go into effect until after the conduct in question. In English, this means Spanier did nothing wrong because there was no law at the time against his action(s).
- On January 22, 2012, Joe Paterno died from lung cancer. At the time of this writing, his lasting legacy is still to be determined.

- Sanctions against Penn State included "Vacating of all wins from 1998 to 2011; 112 wins in all. This had the effect of stripping the Nittany Lions of their shared Big Ten titles in 2005 and 2008. It also removed 112 wins from Paterno's record, dropping him from first to 12th on the NCAA's all-time wins list.

- On January 16, 2015, the NCAA reinstated Paterno's wins.

An article in the American Football Database summarized the events surrounding this scandal as follows. "The scandal had far-reaching outcomes for the university. The report of an independent investigation commissioned by the PSU board and conducted by former FBI director Louis Freeh and his law firm stated that Spanier and Paterno, along with Curley and the school vice president Gary Schultz, had known about allegations of child abuse on Sandusky's part as early as 1998, and were complicit in failing to disclose them. In doing so, Freeh stated that the most senior leaders at Penn State showed a "total disregard for the safety and welfare of Sandusky's child victims" for 14 years and "empowered" Jerry Sandusky to continue his abuse," (https://americanfootballdatabase.fandom.com/wiki/Penn_State_child_sex_abuse_scandal.)

Forensic Leadership Analysis TM.			
Evaluator:			
Organization:			
Leadership Autopsy Toe Tag TM			
Instructions: Check "Yes" if behavior is observable. Check "No" if the behavior is not observable. If behavior is present, circle Value. Add all circled scores together to generate a total score. Compare total score to Evaluation Scale.			
Malignant Behaviors	Observed **Yes**	Value	Observed **No**
Lying		6	
Hubris		6	
Avarice		6	
Duplicity		6	
Cunning		5	
Narcissism		5	
Disconnection		5	
Deception		4	
Dismissiveness		4	
Manipulation		4	
Inconsistency		3	
Unteachability		3	
Gamesmanship		3	
	Total Score		
Evaluation Scale	**Levels**		**Action**
Score 40 - 60	Dying Organization		**Run!**
Score 21 - 39	Malignancy Spreading		**Update Resume**
Score 1 - 20	Malignancy Present		**Observe Closely**

WorldCom

Malignant Leadership Case Study #6

According to Gretchen Morgenson from the New York Times, “Ten former directors of WorldCom, the telecommunications company whose bankruptcy was the largest in history, have agreed to pay $18 million of their own money to settle a class-action lawsuit by investors who lost hundreds of millions of dollars when the company collapsed in July 2002.”

> "New York State has done a great thing for shareholders everywhere," said Greg Taxin, chief executive of Glass Lewis, an institutional investor advisory service in San Francisco. "This may be one of the most important steps toward reinforcing the importance of performing the directorship duties with fidelity toward shareholders. It's going to be very sobering to board members around the country."

Just the Facts

WorldCom was a telecommunications company with its origins dating back to 1983 when it was known as Long Distance Discount Services Inc. (LDDS). In 1985 LDDS would select Bernard Ebbers as its new Chief Executive Officer (CEO).

In 1997 WorldCom would merge with MCI Communications; in 2000, it would formally adopt the name WorldCom. The $37 billion dollar merger was the largest of its kind at the time.

The first signs of trouble manifested themselves between Bernard Ebbers and the Board of Directors. In the early part of 1999, MCI WorldCom was on track to merge with Sprint Corporation. However, the U.S. Justice Department quelled the deal. At the same time, WorldCom stock prices were falling, and the board of Directors needed to stop the bleeding.

It just so happened that at the same time WorldCom stocks were falling "banks were placing increasing demands on Ebbers to cover margin calls on his WorldCom stock that were used to finance his other businesses." Ebbers convinced the Board of Directors to "provide him corporate loans and guarantees," in excess of $400 million dollars. The Board reasoned that if CEO Ebbers were to sell his MCI WorldCom stock, prices would continue to plummet, making the $400 million dollars look like a financial bargain at the time. However, act two of the circus was about to get underway.

The leadership failure which brought about the downfall of WorldCom is rather extensive and complex in its level of deception. Mark Tran, a reporter for the Guardian in his article, WorldCom Accounting Scandal, does an excellent job of chronicling the key leadership failures.

- **The Problem**

"The company said an internal audit had discovered that $3.3 billion in profits were improperly recorded on its books from 1999 to the first quarter of 2002. That is on top of the $3.8 billion in expenses the company said it had improperly reported as capital investments."

- **Accounting Twists**

"WorldCom said most of the $3.3 billion irregularity involved the manipulation of reserves. Companies set aside reserves to cover estimated losses such as uncollected payments from customers and judgements in lawsuits and other expected costs."

- **It's How We Do It.**

"It is a perfectly legitimate practice, like setting aside funds for a rainy day; but reserves can be abused to create the accounting equivalent of a slush fund. If a company wanted to massage profits to meet Wall Street expectations, it can transfer the necessary sums from the reserve. The suspicion is that WorldCom deliberately inflated its reserves to be able to dip into them to boost profits to meet profit projections."

- **It's Not My Fault**

"WorldCom's chief executive, John Sidgmore, blamed the company's former chief financial officer, Scott Sullivan, and the former controller, David Myers. The two were fired for claiming $3.8 billion in regular expenses as capital investment in 2001. The pair were arrested in New York, handcuffed and paraded in front of TV cameras as part of the Bush's administration crackdown on corporate crime. Charged with securities fraud, conspiracy and other charges, they face 65 years in prison. WorldCom's founder and former chief executive, Bernie Ebbers, says he was unaware of the accounting problems, and has not been charged."

- **Who's Watching the Watchers**

“WorldCom's accounting firm at the time were Arthur Andersen, the same company that looked after Enron's books as well as other companies hit by accounting issues - Tyco, Global Crossing, and Adelphia Communications. Andersen accused Mr. Sullivan of withholding information from them. The deputy U.S. Attorney General, Larry Thompson, said: "We have to ask where the professionals were, the accountants, and the lawyers."

- **The Other WorldCom Shoe**

“WorldCom said it may have to write off $50 billion when it restates its finances. One of the largest write-offs in corporate history, that would amount to the 2001 gross domestic products of Hungary and the Czech Republic. Only Time Warner's $54 billion write-off was bigger.”

Bernie Ebbers would turn WorldCom into the second largest telecommunication company in the United States. He would grow WorldCom through a series of acquisitions and leveraging the company’s financial assets to the point breaking. In the end, he will not be remembered for his successes; rather he will be remembered as the CEO who was so bad it took an $11 billion dollar accounting sleight of hand just to hide Ebbers malignant leadership.

Forensic Leadership Analysis ™.

Evaluator:

Organization:

Leadership Autopsy Toe Tag ™

Instructions: Check "Yes" if behavior is observable. Check "No" if the behavior is not observable. If behavior is present, circle Value. Add all circled scores together to generate a total score. Compare total score to Evaluation Scale.

Malignant Behaviors	Observed Yes	Value	Observed No
Lying		6	
Hubris		6	
Avarice		6	
Duplicity		6	
Cunning		5	
Narcissism		5	
Disconnection		5	
Deception		4	
Dismissiveness		4	
Manipulation		4	
Inconsistency		3	
Unteachability		3	
Gamesmanship		3	
	Total Score		

Evaluation Scale	Levels	Action
Score 40 - 60	Dying Organization	**Run!**
Score 21 - 39	Malignancy Spreading	**Update Resume**
Score 1 - 20	Malignancy Present	**Observe Closely**

Wells Fargo

Malignant Leadership Case Study #7

"I don't want our culture to be defined by these mistakes."

Mr. John Stumpf CEO Wells Fargo

Just the Facts

On September 21, 2016, the Corporate Research Project reported, "In September 2016, the CFPB imposed a fine of $100 million against Wells Fargo in connection with the revelation that for years bank employees were creating large numbers of new accounts not requested by customers to generate illicit fees," the announcement would have an immediate impact of the U.S. financial sector as current banking, and most importantly leadership practices are made public.

History of Wells Fargo

From its humble beginnings in 1852 when Henry Wells and William G. Fargo founded the company to provide express (wire money transfer services) and banking services to the residents of California, Wells

Fargo has grown to operate some 8,700 retail branches in 35 countries serving over 70 million customers annually. The allegations of bank employees creating some 2,000,000 fake accounts would seriously challenge Wells Fargo publicly articulated Mission and Vision statement, "Everything we do is built on trust…It's earned relationship by relationship." (Now is a good time to remember that an organizations' actual culture is observed in its actions. It is not garnered from reading their mission or vision statement.)

Until the 1980s, banks mainly took deposits and lent them out to new businesses, which then grew jobs and supported the economy. In the 1970s, for example, the majority of financial flows coming out of the largest U.S. financial institutions went into new business investment. Today, that form of investment represents only 15% of banking services. In 2016 the role of banks in the U.S. had expanded significantly. In 2016, Wells Fargo banking and profit centers included:

- Community Banking
- Consumer Lending
- Private Student Loans
- Wholesale Banking
- Small Business Loans

- Health and Investment Management
- Wells Fargo Securities

Through a series of rapid corporate mergers and purchases that accelerated in the early 1980s, Wells Fargo would become one of the four largest banks in the United States along with J. P. Morgan, Bank of America, and Citigroup. In 2015, Wells Fargo would manage approximately $287 billion in total assets and employ some 265,000 employees globally.

Wells Fargo Executive Leadership 2015 Total Compensation

John Stumpf	$19,300,000
Chairman of the Board and CEO	
John R. Strawberry	$9, 050,000
Timothy J. Sloan	$11,000,000
David M. Carroll	$9,050,000
Avid Modjtabai	$9,050,000
Carrie L. Tolstedt	$9,050,000

In 2015 the leadership Team of Wells Fargo consisted of the following fourteen individuals each earning approximately $300,000 annually.

Wells Fargo 2016 Board Members

John D. Baker II, business executive (director since 2009); director of FRP Holdings.

Elaine L. Chao, Ms. Chao served as the 24th U.S. Secretary of Labor from January 2001 until January 2009.

John S. Chen, served as Executive Chairman and Chief Executive Officer of BlackBerry Limited, Waterloo, Ontario, Canada.

Lloyd H. Dean, served as President, Chief Executive Officer, and a director of Dignity Health, San Francisco, California.

Elizabeth A. Duke, served as a member of the Federal Reserve Board of Governors.

Susan E. Engel, served as Chief Executive Officer of Portero, Inc., New York, New York.

Enrique Hernandez Jr., served as Chairman, President, Chief Executive Officer, and a director of Inter-Con Security Systems, Inc., Pasadena, California.

James M. Donald, served as Chairman and a Director of Vulcan Materials Company, Birmingham, Alabama.

Cynthia H. Milligan, served as Dean of the College of Business Administration at the University of Nebraska-Lincoln, Lincoln, Nebraska

Federico F. Pena, served as a Senior Advisor of Vestar Capital Partners, Denver, Colorado. He served both as the U.S. Secretary of Energy and the U.S. Secretary of Transportation.

James H. Quigley, served as senior partner of Deloitte LLP, New York, New York.

Stephen W. Sanger, served as Chairman of General Mills, Inc., Minneapolis, Minnesota.

Susan G. Swenson, served as a Director of Novatel Wireless.

Suzanne M. Vautrinot, served as President of Kilovolt Consulting Inc., San Antonio, Texas.

Culture is What You Do!

Banking is a business built on trust. In a very real sense, any organization, and especially banks, are only as financially sound and stable as the people responsible for managing them, which is why ethics should be the cornerstone of an experienced and reliable leadership team. At face value, Wells Fargo leadership had an established pattern of highly questionable business practices, which proved to be extremely costly to the bottom line. On September 21, 2016, Phillip Mattera writing for the Corporate Research Project published an article, which lists some of the Wells Fargo business practices leading up to the 2,000,000 phony accounts scandal of 2016.

- In November 2009, it had to agree to buy back $1.4 billion in auction-rate securities to settle allegations by the California attorney general of misleading investors. (https://oag.ca.gov/news/press-releases/brown-recovers-14-billion-wells-fargo-investors-landmark-settlement)

- In May 2011, the Justice Department announced a comprehensive settlement agreement under the Americans with Disabilities Act (ADA) with Wells Fargo & Company to ensure equal access for individuals with disabilities to Wells Fargo's services nationwide. Wells Fargo agreed to pay up to $16 million to settle charges of violating the Americans with Disabilities Act. (https://www.justice.gov/opa/pr/justice-department-reaches-americans-disabilities-act-settlement-wells-fargo)

- In July 2011, Wells Fargo agreed to pay $125 million to settle a lawsuit in which a group of pension funds accused it of misrepresenting the quality of pools of mortgage-related securities. (https://www.nytimes.com/2011/07/08/business/wells-fargo-to-settle-loans-suit.html)

- That same month, the Federal Reserve announced an $85 million civil penalty against Wells Fargo for steering customers with good qualifications into costly subprime mortgage loans during the housing boom.

- In November 2011, Wells Fargo agreed to pay at least $37 million to settle a lawsuit accusing it of municipal bond bid-rigging. (https://www.nytimes.com/2011/11/09/business/wells-fargo-agrees-to-pay-37-million-in-bidding-case.html)

- The following month, FINRA fined it $2 million for improper sales of reverse convertible securities.

- Wells Fargo was one of five large mortgage service providers that, in February 2012, consented to a $25 billion settlement with the federal government and state attorneys general to resolve allegations of loan servicing and foreclosure abuses. (https://www.justice.gov/opa/pr/federal-government-and-state-attorneys-general-reach-25-billion-agreement-five-largest)

- In July 2012, the U.S. Justice Department announced that Wells Fargo would pay $175 million to settle charges that it engaged in a pattern of discrimination against African-American and Hispanic borrowers in its mortgage lending during the period from 2004 to 2009. (Wells Fargo's disgraceful discrimination scandal: A guide The Week Staff) The Justice Department says Wells Fargo engaged in a pattern of "systemic discrimination" in which some 30,000 minority borrowers across 36 states were charged higher fees and interest rates than their white counterparts. (https://www.latimes.com/business/la-xpm-2012-jul-12-fi-mo-wells-bias-20120712-story.html)

- In August 2012, Wells Fargo agreed to pay $6.5 million to settle SEC charges that it failed to fully research the risks associated with mortgage-backed securities before selling them to customers such as municipalities and non-profit organizations. (https://www.sec.gov/news/press-release/2012-2012-155htm)

- In January 2013, Wells Fargo was one of ten major lenders that agreed to pay a total of $8.5 billion to resolve claims of foreclosure abuses. (https://www.occ.gov/news-issuances/news-releases/2013/nr-ia-2013-3.html)

- In October 2013, Freddie Mac announced that Wells Fargo would pay $869 million to repurchase home loans the bank had sold to the mortgage agency that did not conform to the latter's guidelines. (https://www.bloomberg.com/news/articles/2013-09-30/wells-fargo-agrees-to-869-million-settlement-with-freddie-mac)

- In December 2014, FINRA fined Wells Fargo Securities $4 million as part of a case against ten investment banks for allowing their stock analysts to solicit business and offer favorable research coverage in connection with a planned initial public offering of Toys R Us in 2010. (https://www.finra.org/media-center/news-releases/2014/finra-fines-10-firms-total-435-million)

- In March 2016, the SECb charged Wells Fargo with defrauding investors in a municipal bond offering to finance 38 Studios, a Rhode Island startup video game company founded by former Boston Red Sox pitcher Curt Schilling that eventually went bankrupt, leaving the state on the hook for $75 million in debt. (https://www.sec.gov/news/pressrelease/2016-37.html)

- In April 2016, the Justice Department announced that Wells Fargo would pay $1.2 billion to resolve allegations that the bank certified to the Department of Housing and Urban Development that certain residential home mortgage loans were eligible for Federal Housing Administration insurance when they were not, resulting in the government having to pay FHA insurance claims when some of those loans defaulted. (https://www.justice.gov/opa/pr/wells-fargo-bank-agrees-pay-12-billion-improper-mortgage-lending-practices)

- In August 2016, the Consumer Financial Protection Bureau announced that Wells Fargo would pay a penalty of $3.6 million-plus $410,000 in restitution to customers to resolve allegations that it engaged in illegal student loan servicing practices. (https://www.consumerfinance.gov/about-us/newsroom/cfpb-takes-action-against-wells-fargo-illegal-student-loan-servicing-practices/)

This background helps put in perspective why the actions of 5,300 employees, creating some 2,000,000 fraudulent accounts, by Wells Fargo standards could be considered as nothing more than a slight transgression. Given those instances listed above, it is absolutely appropriate and safe to say that Wells Fargo Executive Leadership Team, as well as the Board Members, must not have been familiar with the Wells Fargo Mission Statement,

"Everything we do is built on trust.... It's earned relationship by relationship."

because none of the actions listed above were focused on building trust, relationship by relationship.

The Problem Revealed

"As Mr. Stumpf testified, a video screen on the hearing room's wall displayed a scroll of more than a dozen fines Wells Fargo has paid in recent years, totaling more than $10 billion."

Stacy Crowley

In an article by Matt Egan, September 9, 2016, for CNN Money entitled 5,300 Wells Fargo Employees Fired Over 2 Million Phony Accounts, Egan noted Federal Regulators "stated Wells Fargo (WFC) employees secretly created millions of unauthorized bank and credit card accounts -- without their customers knowing it -- since 2011, submitted applications for 565,443 credit card." These employees were under pressure to open bogus accounts for existing customers then transfer funds "from customers' existing accounts into newly-created ones without their knowledge or consent, regulators say." The CFPB described this practice as "widespread." Customers were being charged for insufficient funds or overdraft fees -- because there wasn't enough money in their original accounts.

When pressed by the senate investigative committee to explain Mr. Stumpf "sought to shift the blame for the mess to relatively low-level employees," responding, "The problem, he explained, was an ethical lapse among the 5,300 employees, most of them low-level bankers and tellers, who had been fired for their actions since 2011. Stumpf also said, "The 1% that did it wrong, who we fired, terminated, in no way reflects our culture."

His message did not resonate well with members of the House Financial Service Committee, who were even angrier and more hostile by his responses than their Senate counterparts who questioned him earlier. "Democrats and Republicans alike took turns ripping apart Mr. Stumpf and what took place at the bank he leads. They denounced the actions as "theft," "a criminel enterprise," identity fraud, an outrage, and a devastating blow to the entire banking industry."

At the same time, Capitol Hill was putting pressure on Mr. Stumpf for answers and guarantees of meaningful reform; previous Wells Fargo employees were telling their personal stories of the abuse, harassment, and unethical business practices they had observed.

"They ruined my life, "Bill Bado, a former Wells Fargo banker in Pennsylvania, told CNNMoney. Bado not only refused orders to open phony bank and credit accounts, the New Jersey man called an ethics hotline and sent an email to human resources in September 2013, flagging unethical sales activities he was being instructed to do.

Eight days after that email, a copy of which CNNMoney obtained, Bado was terminated. The stated reason, Tardiness."

"Another six former Wells Fargo employees told CNNMoney they witnessed similar behavior at Wells Fargo -- even though the company has a policy in place that is supposed to prevent retaliation against whistleblowers."

"Heather Brock, the business banker from Texas, told CNNMoney she experienced a similar situation. The 26-year-old single parent of two young boys was fired soon after she contacted the company's ethics line about illegal sales practices she witnessed."

> "One former Wells Fargo human resources official even said the bank had a method in place to retaliate against tipsters. He said that Wells Fargo would find ways to fire employees "in retaliation for shining light" on sales issues. It could be as simple as monitoring the employee to find a fault, like showing up a few minutes late on several occasions."

As Emily Glazer notes in her article, Carrie Tolstedt: In the Eye of the Wells Fargo Storm, the idea that 5,300 employees could act without knowledge of Carrie Tolstedt is highly unlikely, "Inside Wells Fargo & Co., some executives called Carrie Tolstedt "the watchmaker" for her obsessive attention to detail in running the firm's sprawling retail-banking operation." However, Ms. Tolstedt wasn't asked to appear at the congressional hearing. She stepped down from her post atop the retail-banking business in July and planned to retire at the end of the year. As a part of her retirement package, in addition to the $27 million she earned in the three previous years, she will also retire with an estimated $125 million in stock and options.

CEO John Stumpf sums up her performance as follows, "she had performed well in other duties like branding and improving customer loyalty, which he said were "top of class" among large banks."

One Final Ripple

Wells Fargo's broken culture persists as reposted by Jackie Wattles on September 30, 2016, in her article entitled *Wells Fargo Illegally Repossessed 413 Service Members' Cars*. "Wells Fargo will pay $24 million to settle allegations it mistreated members of the military, including illegally repossessing their cars."

- The Justice Department said the illegal repossessions took place from 2008 to 2015.

- The bank was fined $20 million more by the Office of the Comptroller of the Currency for breaking three provisions of the same law by denying members of the military certain banking protections, including capping their interest rates at 6%. Those violations began in 2006, the OCC said.

- Wells Fargo said in a statement that it apologizes for not living up to its commitment of ensuring that all service members "receive the appropriate benefits and protections."

In the end, John Stumpf never could grasp the reality that he was the wrong man for the job. Mr. Stumpf told Jim Cramer in an interview on Mad Money, "I think the best thing I could do right now is lead this company, and lead this company forward," proving that not only are malignant leaders unteachable, they are also resistant to change.

Post Script

On October 12, 2016, Dan Freed and Elizabeth Dilt, from Reuters, reported that Wells Fargo "CEO John Stumph abruptly resigned." He was replaced by his long-time Chief Operating Officer Timothy Sloan. The same Timothy J. Sloan, who in 2015 was paid $11,000,000 for his contribution in helping to make Wells Fargo what it was. The Wells Fargo Board, in its infinite wisdom, decided that Mr. Sloan was the breath of fresh air that Wells Fargo needed to fix all the problems. As Forensic Leadership Pathologists, we can predict, with a high degree of reliability, the chances of meaningful systemic change occurring at Wells Fargo under this new leadership is practically non-existent.

In the future, I predict Wells Fargo will no longer exist as it does in early 2020. The malignant culture that drives the organization is so pervasive, and not in a good way, that there is no way to stop Wells Fargo from imploding; when it does, it's going to be a world-class fire sale. You don’t have to be an oracle to see this inevitable train wreck in the making.

Forensic Leadership Analysis TM.			
Evaluator:			
Organization:			
Leadership Autopsy Toe Tag TM			
Instructions: Check "Yes" if behavior is observable. Check "No" if the behavior is not observable. If behavior is present, circle Value. Add all circled scores together to generate a total score. Compare total score to Evaluation Scale.			
Malignant Behaviors	Observed **Yes**	Value	Observed **No**
Lying		6	
Hubris		6	
Avarice		6	
Duplicity		6	
Cunning		5	
Narcissism		5	
Disconnection		5	
Deception		4	
Dismissiveness		4	
Manipulation		4	
Inconsistency		3	
Unteachability		3	
Gamesmanship		3	
	Total Score		

Evaluation Scale	**Levels**	**Action**
Score 40 - 60	Dying Organization	**Run!**
Score 21 - 39	Malignancy Spreading	**Update Resume**
Score 1 - 20	Malignancy Present	**Observe Closely**

Enron

Malignant Leadership Case Study #8

> "Through my whole life, I have lived my life in such a way to make sure that I never violate any law…certainly never any criminal laws…and always maintained that most important to me was my integrity, was my character, were my values."
>
> *Kenneth Lay*

Just the Facts

Kenneth Lay, like so many failing leaders of today, simply refused to grasp the concept that culture is what you do. Culture is not what you *say*, it is not what you *think*, and it is most certainly not what you *believe* to be true.

- Enron was once ranked the sixth-largest energy company in the world.

- Enron paid the top 140 executives $680 million in 2001. In 2001 Kenneth Lay received $67.4 million, and Jeffrey Skilling received $41.8 million in financial compensation. Both men were incredibly well paid.

- At their peak in August 2000 Enron shares were worth $90.75. By January 2000 the value of Enron stock had dropped to $0.67 a share. At 67¢ a share Enron had achieved junk bond status.

- Top Enron executives sold their company stock prior to the company's downfall.

- Lower-level employees were prevented from selling their stock due to 401k restrictions, and many subsequently lost their life savings.

- Most of the top executives were tried for fraud after it was revealed in November 2001 that Enron's earnings had been overstated by several hundred million dollars.

Kenneth Lay and Jeffrey Skilling were just your typical CEO's. The two will forever be linked together for their gross malfeasance and complete absence of ethics, however, all that said, the important thing to remember is this, they are more similar to leaders of business and industry today than they are dissimilar.

Kenneth Lay was the CEO and Chairman of Enron. Originally, Enron specialized in the transmission and distribution of electricity and natural gas throughout the United States. It expanded its services to include the building and management of pipelines and power plants, fiber optics, data management, and telecommunications holding. In its heyday, "Enron employed approximately 20,000 staff and was one of the world's major electricity, natural gas, communications, and pulp and paper companies, claiming revenues of nearly $101 billion in 2000."

Earlier in his career, Lay was the Undersecretary for the Department of the Interior before returning to private industry to leverage what he had learned. He was a close friend to the Bush family, was extremely active in the Republican Party, and was co-chairman of the 1992 re-elect Bush campaign. He was so well connected politically that in 2000 he was mentioned as a possible candidate for the Secretary of the Treasury.

In 1994 Kenneth Lay was one of the highest-paid CEO's in the nation earning more than $42 million dollars annually. Yet during his trial in 2006, he would report to the court a net worth of negative $250,000, despite liquidating over $300 million in stocks between 1998 and 2001.

The Enron bankruptcy was the largest of its kind in the history of the United States. Proof once more that sheer size and revenues, $101 billion annually, cannot save even the largest companies from malignant leadership, "Enron used a variety of deceptive, bewildering, and fraudulent accounting practices and tactics to cover its fraud in reporting Enron's financial information," (https://en.wikipedia.org/wiki/Enron). Not only did 20,000 employees lose their jobs, but investors lost an estimated $60 billion dollars along with an additional $2.1 billion in private pension plans.

The Enron accounting scandals would ultimately play a significant role in causing the demise of Arthur Andersen, the fifth-largest U.S. accounting firm at the time. The Chicago Tribune summed up the entire failure of Arthur Anderson to remain objective in the article, Ties to Enron Blinded Andersen, when they reported the following:

> "Their paychecks came from Anderson, but their livelihoods depended on the fast-growing darling of Wall Street. Enron could be a volatile partner, at times, even a bully. But Andersen was hooked on

a relationship that it found simply too lucrative to abandon.

“Many of Andersen and Enron's top number crunchers took annual golf vacations together, making friendly bets on each round. They went on ski outings, schussing down the slopes together. Others would sneak away from the office for Astros games at Enron Field. They played fantasy football against each other over the office computers.

"It was like these very bright geeks at Andersen suddenly got invited to this really cool, macho frat party," said Leigh Anne Dear, a former senior audit manager at Andersen who worked in Enron tower. "They were out of control, and they didn't even know it because it was so cool to associate yourself with the top, with the guys who run a multi-billion-dollar company.”

“In time, insiders at both disgraced firms now say, those close ties eroded the most important role Andersen was supposed to play as Enron's auditor: providing strong, independent verification of its financial reports.”

In 2000, Arthur Andersen billed Enron for $58 million dollars in services. In the end, the relationship simply involved too much money to remain objective. Ultimately Sherron Watkins, the former Vice President of Corporate Development, would testify before the United States House of Representative and Senate regarding her understanding of the Enron's creative accounting practices. Her testimony would show that Enron was cooking the books to project themselves as something they most definitely were not, financially solvent. Below is an abbreviated timeline developed by CNN, of Enron activities.

Enron Timeline of Activities:
July 1985 - Enron is formed by the merger of Houston Natural Gas and Omaha-based InterNorth.

2000 - Enron reaches No. 7 on the Fortune 500 list.

August 14, 2001 - Skilling resigns as CEO, and Lay becomes CEO again. (He had been CEO from 1985-2000)

August 15, 2001 - Sherron Watkins sends a memo to Lay about accounting issues.

October 16, 2001 - Enron announces a third-quarter loss of $618 million.

October 31, 2001 - The SEC opens a formal investigation into Enron's transactions.

December 2, 2001 - Enron files for Chapter 11 protection, becoming the largest bankruptcy in U.S. history, leaving thousands of workers with worthless stock.

January 9, 2002 - The U.S. Department of Justice opens a criminal investigation into Enron's collapse.

January 11, 2002 - The SEC widens its investigation to include Enron's chief auditor, Arthur Andersen, due to reports of document shredding.

January 15, 2002 - The NYSE suspends trading of Enron shares.

January 17, 2002 - Enron ends its partnership with Arthur Andersen.

January 23, 2002 - Lay resigns as chairman of the board and CEO.

January 25, 2002 - Former Enron Vice-chairman J. Clifford Baxter commits suicide in Sugar Land, Texas.

February 7, 2002 - Andrew Fastow, Michael Kopper, Richard Buy, and Richard Causey all invoke their Fifth Amendment rights before the House Energy and Commerce Committee.

February 12, 2002 - Lay invokes his Fifth Amendment right before the Senate Commerce Committee.

February 14, 2002 - Whistleblower Watkins testifies before the House of Representatives.

March 14, 2002 – U.S. Justice Department indicts accounting firm Arthur Andersen for obstruction of justice in the Enron case.

June 15, 2002 - Arthur Andersen is found guilty of obstructing justice.

August 21, 2002 - Former Enron executive Kopper pleads guilty to conspiracy to commit wire fraud and money laundering conspiracy.

October 2, 2002 - Fastow is charged with securities fraud, wire fraud, mail fraud, money laundering, and conspiracy.

May 1, 2003 - Fastow, his wife, and seven others are charged in a superseding indictment for actions relating to the firm's financial scandals.

January 14, 2004 - Fastow and his wife each plead guilty as part of a plea agreement.

January 22, 2004 - Causey pleads not guilty to five counts of securities fraud and one count of conspiracy to commit securities fraud.

February 19, 2004 - Former Enron CEO Skilling is indicted on fraud and conspiracy charges and pleads not guilty.

May 6, 2004 - Lea Fastow pleads guilty to a single count of filing a false tax return and receives a 12-month sentence.

May 19, 2004 - The former Enron vice president responsible for investor relations, Paula Rieker, pleads guilty to insider trading.

July 7, 2004 - Lay is indicted on 11 counts - one count of conspiracy to commit security and wire fraud, two counts of wire fraud for misleading statements at employee meetings, four counts of securities fraud for false statements in presentations to securities analysts, one count of bank fraud, and three counts of making false statements to banks.

July 8, 2004 - Lay pleads not guilty to all 11 charges and is released on $500,000 unsecured bond.

November 17, 2004 - Enron comes out of bankruptcy after selling its interest in three natural gas pipelines to CCE Holdings for $2 billion.

May 31, 2005 - The U.S. Supreme Court overturns Arthur Andersen's obstruction of justice conviction.

December 28, 2005 - Causey pleads guilty to securities fraud for his role in the Enron scandal. He will serve only seven years in exchange for cooperating with prosecutors seeking convictions of his former bosses, Lay and Skilling.

March 28, 2006 - The judge dismisses three counts against Skilling (two charges of securities fraud and one charge of lying to auditors) and one count of securities fraud against Lay.

May 25, 2006 - The jury in the Enron case finds former CEO Skilling and founder Lay guilty of conspiracy and fraud. Lay is convicted of all six counts against him, and Skilling is found guilty on 19 counts of conspiracy, fraud, false statements, and insider trading. Skilling is found not guilty on nine counts of insider trading. Judge Simeon T. Lake announces four guilty verdicts in the separate bench trial of Lay on separate counts of conspiracy and fraud.

July 5, 2006 - Lay dies in Aspen, Colorado, from a heart attack brought on by severe coronary artery disease.

September 26, 2006 - Fastow is sentenced to six years in prison, four years less than his plea agreement stipulated in January 2004.

October 23, 2006 - Skilling is sentenced to 24 years and four months in prison.

November 15, 2006 - Former COO Causey is sentenced to five years and six months in prison for one count of securities fraud.

November 16, 2006 - Skilling appeals his convictions to the 5th Circuit Court of Appeals.

December 13, 2006 - Skilling reports to prison in Waseca, Minnesota, after a judge refuses to allow him to remain free pending appeal.

January 3, 2007 - Causey reports to the Bastrop Federal Correctional Institution to begin serving his five-and-a-half-year sentence.

January 6, 2009 - The U.S. Court of Appeals affirms Skilling's conviction but sends his case back for re-sentencing.

June 24, 2010 - The U.S. Supreme Court rules that Skilling was incorrectly prosecuted under a law concerning "honest-services fraud." The court then nullifies Skilling's conviction on that charge.

April 6, 2011 - The Fifth U.S. Circuit Court of Appeals confirms Skilling's criminal conviction.

May 16, 2011 - Fastow is transferred from a federal prison in Louisiana to a halfway house in Houston. He is later allowed to move to his home to complete his sentence.

May 17, 2011 - Causey begins serving the rest of his five-and-a-half-year sentence in home confinement.

April 16, 2012 - The U.S. Supreme Court turns aside Skilling's second appeal. A few weeks later, Skilling's attorney files a motion requesting a new trial in Houston federal court citing newly discovered evidence.

June 21, 2013 - A federal judge reduces Skilling's sentence by more than 10 years. As part of the re-sentencing deal brokered between prosecutors and the defense, Skilling agrees to stop challenging his conviction and forfeit roughly $42 million that will be distributed among the victims of the Enron fraud.

November 18, 2015 - A federal judge issues a ruling that bars Skilling from ever acting as an officer or director of a publicly traded company again, settling a long-running civil suit by the U.S. Securities Exchange Commission.

March 1, 2017 - A federal judge dismisses a class action lawsuit against UBS, accused of hiding fraud committed by Enron, a former client.

Forensic Leadership Analysis ™.			
Evaluator:			
Organization:			
Leadership Autopsy Toe Tag ™			
Instructions: Check "Yes" if behavior is observable. Check "No" if the behavior is not observable. If behavior is present, circle Value. Add all circled scores together to generate a total score. Compare total score to Evaluation Scale.			
Malignant Behaviors	Observed **Yes**	Value	Observed **No**
Lying		6	
Hubris		6	
Avarice		6	
Duplicity		6	
Cunning		5	
Narcissism		5	
Disconnection		5	
Deception		4	
Dismissiveness		4	
Manipulation		4	
Inconsistency		3	
Unteachability		3	
Gamesmanship		3	
	Total Score		
Evaluation Scale	**Levels**		**Action**
Score 40 - 60	Dying Organization		**Run!**
Score 21 - 39	Malignancy Spreading		**Update Resume**
Score 1 - 20	Malignancy Present		**Observe Closely**

Crazy Eddie

Malignant Leadership Case Study #9

The following case study was taken in its entirety from Wikipedia March, 2020, https://en.wikipedia.org/wiki/Crazy_Eddie.

"Crazy Eddie was a consumer electronics chain in the Northeastern United States. The chain was started in 1971 in Brooklyn, New York, by businessmen Eddie and Sam M. Antar, and was previously named ERS Electronics (ERS stood for Eddie, Rose and Sam; Rose and Sam were Eddie's parents). The chain rose to prominence throughout the Tri-State Region as much for its prices as for its memorable radio and television commercials, featuring a frenetic, "crazy" character played by radio DJ Jerry Carroll (who copied most of his shtick from early TV-commercial pioneer, used car and electronics salesman Earl "Madman" Muntz). At its peak, Crazy Eddie had 43 stores in four states, and reported more than $300 million in sales.

Unable to sustain his fraudulent business practices, co-founder Eddie Antar cashed in millions of dollars' worth of stock and resigned from the company in December 1986. Crazy Eddie's board of directors approved the sale of the company in November 1987. The entire Antar family was immediately removed from the business. The new owners quickly discovered the true extent of the Antar family's fraud, but were unable to turn around Crazy Eddie's quickly declining fortunes. In 1989, the company declared bankruptcy and was liquidated.

In February 1987, the United States Attorney's Office for the District of New Jersey commenced a federal grand jury investigation into the financial activities of Crazy Eddie. In September of that year, the United States Securities and Exchange Commission initiated an investigation into alleged violations of federal securities laws by certain Crazy Eddie officers and employees. Eddie Antar was eventually charged with a series of crimes. Antar fled to Israel in February 1990, but was returned to the United States in January 1993 to stand trial. His 1993 conviction on fraud charges was overturned, but he eventually pleaded guilty in 1996. In 1997, Antar was sentenced to eight years in prison and was subject to numerous fines. He was released from prison in 1999.

Eddie Antar's grandparents, Murad and Tera Antar, who were Syrian Jews, relocated to Brooklyn,

New York from Aleppo, Syria. Murad and Tera worked in their market stalls alongside Arabs, including Egyptians, other Syrians, as well as Turks. Eddie's father Sam Antar was a retailer, and it was no surprise to the family that Eddie also became a retailer.

The predecessor to Crazy Eddie was a consumer electronics shop called Sight and Sound. It was a property of ERS Electronics, a company owned by Sam M. Antar, his son Eddie Antar, and Eddie's cousin Ronnie Gindi. Sight and Sound, located on Kings Highway in Brooklyn, began operation in 1969 and offered electronics at regular prices. Due to his aggressive sales techniques, Eddie quickly became known as "Crazy Eddie," but within eighteen months, the shop (as well as Eddie and Ronnie) was nearly bankrupt. Eddie bought out Gindi's one-third ownership stake of Sight and Sound, and Sam M. Antar retained his one-third stake but left the day-to-day operations to Eddie. In 1971, the Sight and Sound store on Kings Highway was renamed Crazy Eddie. Eddie continued his sales tactics with the renamed Crazy Eddie shop, but this time was successful. Eventually, Eddie closed that location and relocated the business to a bigger shop, just a few blocks from Sight and Sound's old location. In 1973, Antar opened the second Crazy Eddie location in Syosset, New York. A third followed during 1975, located in Manhattan. That year, Antar established a main corporate office in Brooklyn, New York. The list of locations were Manhattan, Bronx, Brooklyn, Syosset, Paramus, East Brunswick, Union, Westchester, Westbury, and Norwalk CT.

Antar bought advertising space on New York radio station WPIX-FM. In 1972, a live commercial was performed by DJ "Dr. Jerry" Carroll, who ended the scene by reading the shop's slogan, “his prices are insane,” in this manner: "Crazy Eddie, his prices are IN-SA-A-A-A-ANE!" Antar telephoned and told Carroll to say the line the same way every time, and thus a working relationship had begun.

Beginning in 1975, Carroll began television advertisements. For most of the next fifteen years, Carroll performed commercials in the same frenetic manner he had for radio. One of his more memorable promotions was for Crazy Eddie's annual “Christmas in August” sale, where he would dress in a Santa suit and do the commercial while stagehands threw fake snowballs at him. Carroll also had a trademark look in each commercial, wearing a blue suit with a lighter blue turtleneck shirt in almost all of his appearances. Carroll even appeared in a Spanish-language Crazy Eddie advertisement, although he did not have a speaking role; instead, his appearance consisted of him holding a radio to his ear as he walked behind the commercial's spokesman, stopping only to wave at the camera several times.

During the 1980s, more than 7,500 unique radio and television ads were broadcast in the tri-state area. Carroll's acting became so identified with the company that many people thought he was actually Crazy Eddie; Crazy Eddie even made a commercial to this effect with Carroll as a Superman-styled superhero named Crazy Eddie. Warner Communications, the parent company of the distributor of the *Superman* movie series, found the commercial to be problematic and sued the chain trying to stop it. At the time, Warner also was the parent company of the Atari video game company, and its largest customer for systems and games was Crazy Eddie. Therefore, in retaliation for the lawsuit, Eddie said that if Warner was going to sue for the commercial, he would stop selling Atari products in his stores. The suit was eventually settled.

Almost from the beginning, Crazy Eddie's management engaged in various forms of fraud. The Antars deliberately falsified their books to reduce (or eliminate) their taxable income. They also paid employees off the books, and regularly skimmed thousands of dollars (in cash) earned at the shops. For every $5 Crazy Eddie reported as income, $1 was taken by the Antars. In 1979, the Antars began depositing much of this money—hundreds of thousands of dollars—in Israeli bank accounts. The Antar family skimmed an estimated $3 to $4 million per year at the height of their fraud. In one offshore bank account, the family deposited more than $6 million between 1980 and 1983.[3]

By 1983, it was becoming more and more difficult to hide the millions of illicit dollars. The Antars decided that the way to cover up their growing fraud was to take the company public. In preparation, Eddie initiated a scheme in 1979 to skim less each year. Since more income was actually being reported, this had the effect of showing drastically increasing profit margins. While the company's actual profits (taking into account skimmed profits) from 1980 to 1983 increased approximately 13%, reported profits increased nearly 171%.[9]

Despite the misgivings of people closely associated with Crazy Eddie, the company held its initial public offering on September 13, 1984 (former symbol: CRZY). Shares of the company sold initially for $8. By early 1986, Crazy Eddie stock was trading at more than $75 per share.

Eddie recruited his cousin, Sam E. Antar (known as Sammy), to assist the company with its fraud. Sammy earned a degree in accounting in 1980, and served his apprenticeship with Penn and Horowitz. In 1986, he was named chief financial officer of the company. Sammy was informed that there was a $3 million deficit from the previous year's inventory fraud that needed to be hidden. Additionally, he was instructed to find ways to show a 10% growth in sales. One of Sammy's major schemes was a money laundering operation later known as the Panama Pump, money that the Antars had deposited in Israeli banks was transferred to bank accounts in Panama. These accounts, opened using false names, then drafted payments to Crazy Eddie. This money was largely used to inflate same-store sales totals for the company.

As a public company, Eddie, Sammy, and others engaged in increasing amounts of inventory fraud to increase reported profits and inflate the value of Crazy Eddie stock. For the fiscal year ended March 1, 1985, Crazy Eddie falsified inventories by $3 million. The next fiscal year, that amount increased to between $10 and $12 million.

Collapse

Only months after Crazy Eddie's IPO, Eddie started arguing with his wife and former high school sweetheart, Debbie. He began having an affair with another, younger woman, also named Debbie. They were caught by Eddie's wife and sister on New Year's Eve 1984. Crazy Eddie's troubles began almost immediately afterward; the scam had relied extensively on family members helping keep the appearance that it was an immensely successful company.

By 1987, Sammy's goal was no longer to show greater profitability, but rather to disguise previous frauds. During fiscal year 1987, they falsified inventories between \$22.5 and \$28 million. In addition, Crazy Eddie booked \$20 million in phony debit memos or charge backs to vendors that reduced accounts payable.

As the company's fraud became more difficult to disguise, the public perception of Crazy Eddie as a commercial success began to change. By October 1986, the company's stock value had decreased to \$17.50 per share. During December, Eddie announced his resignation as president and CEO. In April 1987, it was announced that Eddie had in fact retained his role as president but had dismissed, among others, his father Sam M. Antar. But by then, Eddie had already cashed out his share of Crazy Eddie stock, worth between \$25 million and \$30 million.

By the spring of 1987, the company's stock cost less than \$10 a share. Additionally, earnings decreased 20% from the previous year. The franchise did show a

34% sales increase, but this was mainly the result of 13 new store openings. In May 1987, Eddie began proceedings to make the company a privately held company again.[12]

Before that could happen, Houston-based businessman Elias Zinn and management consultant Victor Palmieri initiated a hostile takeover. With Palmieri's backing, Zinn purchased $17.5 million worth of Crazy Eddie stock, which represented 7.5% of the outstanding shares. Once rumors of a takeover started, financial analysts began to examine more closely Crazy Eddie's financial situation. What they discovered was that while most stockholders of the company had lost money since 1984, Eddie had sold 6.5 million shares worth $74 million. A flurry of stockholder lawsuits was filed against the Antar family.[3]

Eddie and Sammy briefly attempted to counter-offer Zinn's takeover, but Zinn quickly topped their funds. The Antars' bid was ended, and Zinn became the new owner of Crazy Eddie on November 6, 1987. He immediately dismissed the rest of the Antar family from any important jobs. When Palmieri's financial analysts completed their preliminary audit a few weeks after the takeover, they estimated that Crazy Eddie's inventory was short by $40 to $50 million. The final figure was $80 million.

By June 1988, Crazy Eddie's suppliers were demanding the liquidation of the company, so they could recover money owed to them; in 1989 they got their wish. The closing of Crazy Eddie began in March 1989, as the company shuttered 17 of its 43 stores. On June 6, 1989, Crazy Eddie was served with a petition by five of its creditors, who had not been paid a total of $860,000 they were owed, which sought to have the company forced into bankruptcy. The company originally planned to fight the petition and file for dismissal, but 15 days later, Crazy Eddie voluntarily filed for Chapter 11 bankruptcy protection. Company president and CEO Peter Martosella cited problems created by the creditors' position (which he termed "ill-advised"), but said business would be conducted as usual at the remaining 26 stores and that Crazy Eddie was still a strong franchise. The company vowed to stay in business but despite Martosella's assertions, Crazy Eddie continued to falter. By the autumn of 1989, sales were continuing to decrease and stores were unable to keep items stocked due to lack of supplier interest in the company. Faced with these facts, Crazy Eddie management decided that the chain was not worth saving. Soon after Crazy Eddie began going-out-of-business sales, but store supply remained minimal even when leftover merchandise from stores that had shuttered was sent to others that were still in operation. By the end of 1989 the remaining 26 Crazy Eddie locations closed and the chain ceased to exist. During a period of three years, Crazy Eddie had gone from one of the most lucrative retailers in the United States, trading at $75 per share, to bankruptcy and liquidation.

Legal Battles

In the meantime, a longtime Crazy Eddie associate named Arnie Spindler, who quit the company after Eddie dismissed his father Sam, brothers Allen and Mitchell and others after a family dispute, had provided investigators with information concerning Crazy Eddie's fraudulent business practices. Spindler implicated Eddie and Sammy, but stated the rest of the family was innocent, though subpoenas were served to the entire Antar family.

Based on information gathered during its investigation, the SEC charged Eddie Antar with securities fraud and illegal insider trading on September 6, 1989. In January 1990, a Federal district judge ordered Antar to repatriate more than $50 million he had transferred illegally to Israel. He was also ordered to appear in court to explain what had happened with the money. When he failed to appear, an arrest warrant was issued. Eddie surrendered to U.S. Marshals a week later, but was released and ordered to appear at a second hearing. When he failed to appear at that hearing, a second arrest warrant was issued, and his assets were frozen.[3]

Eddie fled to Israel using a fake passport and the alias David Jacob Levi Cohen, and purchased a townhouse in the city of Yavne. After Eddie fled the country, Sammy offered to testify for Federal prosecutors in exchange for immunity. Sammy pleaded guilty to three felonies. He avoided jail time in exchange for his testimony, however, and was instead sentenced to six months of house arrest, 1,200 hours of community service, three years of probation, and was levied more than $10,000 in fines. As of 2009, Sammy was an adviser for government agencies and businesses investigating fraud.

Eddie was arrested in June 1992 on federal racketeering conspiracy charges and was extradited to the United States in January 1993. He pleaded not guilty and his trial began in June 1993, and was prosecuted jointly by U.S. Attorneys Paul Weissman and Michael Chertoff. On July 20, Eddie was found guilty of seventeen counts of fraud. His brother, Mitchell, was found guilty of three counts, and acquitted on two. Eddie was sentenced to 12½ years in prison. The Antars' lawyers immediately filed an appeal, citing what they believed was bias on the part of the presiding judge. In April 1995, the verdicts against Eddie and Mitchell were overturned by a Federal appeals panel. Chertoff, calling Eddie "the Darth Vader of capitalism," vowed to begin a new trial.

Eddie Antar eventually pleaded guilty to federal fraud charges in May 1996. In February 1997, he was sentenced to eight years in prison. He was also ordered to pay more than $150 million in fines, in addition to the more than $1 billion in judgments against him resulting from various civil suits. Efforts to recover additional money from the Antar family on behalf of defrauded stockholders were completed in 2012." (Taken verbatim from Wikipedia March,
2020, https://en.wikipedia.org/wiki/Crazy_Eddie)

Forensic Leadership Analysis TM.			
Evaluator:			
Organization:			
Leadership Autopsy Toe Tag TM			
Instructions: Check "Yes" if behavior is observable. Check "No" if the behavior is not observable. If behavior is present, circle Value. Add all circled scores together to generate a total score. Compare total score to Evaluation Scale.			
Malignant Behaviors	Observed **Yes**	Value	Observed **No**
Lying		6	
Hubris		6	
Avarice		6	
Duplicity		6	
Cunning		5	
Narcissism		5	
Disconnection		5	
Deception		4	
Dismissiveness		4	
Manipulation		4	
Inconsistency		3	
Unteachability		3	
Gamesmanship		3	
	Total Score		

Evaluation Scale	**Levels**	**Action**
Score 40 - 60	Dying Organization	**Run!**
Score 21 - 39	Malignancy Spreading	**Update Resume**
Score 1 - 20	Malignancy Present	**Observe Closely**

Theranos

Malignant Leadership Case Study #10

At the age of 19, Elizabeth Holmes dropped out of Stanford University to launch a new blood testing procedure that was going to revolutionize the health care industry. According to Investopedia August 27, 2019, "Theranos Inc., a consumer healthcare technology startup, was once valued at $10 billion, and its leadership claimed it would revolutionize the blood-testing industry. However, the technological breakthrough that CEO Elizabeth Holmes and former company president Ramesh Balwani touted was never demonstrated, and the assertions of Holmes and Balwani amounted to outright deceit. Holmes and Balwani were ultimately charged by the SEC for massive fraud. (https://www.investopedia.com/articles/investing/020116/theranos-fallen-unicorn.asp)

This timeline chronicles the rapid rise of Theranos

- 2003 Elizabeth Holmes, a chemical engineering student, drops out of Stanford to form Theranos.

- 2007 Holmes manages to secure roughly $50 million of funding from investors.
- 2010 The company Theranos was valued by Wall Street at $1 billion dollars. Theranos was a company on the fast track.
- 2014 Elizabeth Holmes had secured close to $400 million in total funding, and the company was valued at roughly $9 billion dollars.
- 2015 Blue Cross of Pennsylvania contracts with Theranos as their preferred lab provider.
- October 2015, The Wall Street Journal reports on inherent performance concerns regarding Theranos. “Based on interviews with ex-employees, the newspaper alleged rampant management incompetence and claimed that Theranos had grossly exaggerated the capabilities of its proprietary technology. One former senior employee stated that only a small fraction of all the tests were conducted on the "Edison machines," and the majority of tests were handled on competitors' equipment despite Theranos's claims to the contrary.” (https://www.investopedia.com/articles/investing/020116/theranos-fallen-unicorn.asp)

- Eleven days later, The Wall Street Journal would go on to report, “The FDA released two partially-redacted Form 483 reports from an ongoing investigation into Theranos. The reports were less than favorable and claimed that Theranos had "uncleared medical device(s)," poor records, was mishandling complaints, and had failed to conduct audits and produce supplier qualifications. In regard to an unspecified medical device, an investigator noted "the design was not validated under actual or simulated use conditions." Further, Theranos failed to “ensure the device conforms to defined user needs and intended uses.”
- May 2017 “Theranos settled a lawsuit with Partner Fund Management, one of its largest investors, after the hedge fund accused the company of securities fraud.”
- May 2018 “The SEC charged Theranos, its founder and CEO Elizabeth Holmes, and its former President Ramesh "Sunny" Balwani with massive fraud. The complaint alleged that the company raised more than $700 million by deceiving investors for years about the company's performance. Both Theranos and Holmes agreed to settle the fraud charges pending court approval.”

(https://www.investopedia.com/articles/investing/020116/theranos-fallen-unicorn.asp)

- June 2018, "A federal grand jury indicted both Holmes and Balwani on nine counts of wire fraud and two counts of conspiracy to commit wire fraud." (Zaw Thina Tun, Investopedia August 27, 2019)

When asked to explain how the Theranos' testing procedures actually worked, Holmes was less then forth coming in her response, replying, "a chemistry is performed so that a chemical reaction occurs and generates a signal from the chemical interaction with the sample, which is translated into a result, which is then reviewed by certified laboratory personnel."

Kate Clark, a reporter for techcrunch.com provides an excellent summery of the rise and fall of Theranos in her story, Theranos Founder Elizabeth Holmes to stand trial in 2020, dated June 28, 2019.

> "Theranos, founded in 2003 by then 19-year-old Stanford dropout Holmes, raised more than $700 million from private market investors in what's been referred to by the Securities and Exchange Commission as an "elaborate, years-long fraud in which they exaggerated or made false statements

about the company's technology, business, and financial performance.

"Holmes and former Theranos president Ramesh "Sunny" Balwani were indicted by a grand jury last June (2020) with 11 criminal charges in total. Two of those charges were conspiracy to commit wire fraud (against investors, and against doctors and patients). The remaining nine are actual wire fraud, with amounts ranging from the cost of a lab test to $100 million.

In light of all the evidence, Elizabeth Holmes maintains her innocence and is awaiting trial at the time of this printing.

Forensic Leadership Analysis ™.

Evaluator:

Organization:

Leadership Autopsy Toe Tag ™

Instructions: Check "Yes" if behavior is observable. Check "No" if the behavior is not observable. If behavior is present, circle Value. Add all circled scores together to generate a total score. Compare total score to Evaluation Scale.

Malignant Behaviors	Observed **Yes**	Value	Observed **No**
Lying		6	
Hubris		6	
Avarice		6	
Duplicity		6	
Cunning		5	
Narcissism		5	
Disconnection		5	
Deception		4	
Dismissiveness		4	
Manipulation		4	
Inconsistency		3	
Unteachability		3	
Gamesmanship		3	
	Total Score		

Evaluation Scale	**Levels**	**Action**
Score 40 - 60	Dying Organization	**Run!**
Score 21 - 39	Malignancy Spreading	**Update Resume**
Score 1 - 20	Malignancy Present	**Observe Closely**

The purpose of these case studies is to provide an opportunity to gain experience observing various magnitudes of malignant leadership behaviors in action. By now, you have probably realized that not all malignant leaders are equal. Some, as illustrated through these examples, are far worse than others. However, the one thing malignant leaders all have in common is their ability to destroy even the healthiest organization single-handedly. No matter how many zeros a business may have on its balance sheet, no matter how talented an organization's employees may be, and regardless of how long a company may have been in business when a malignant leader negatively alters the culture of an organization, they set the wheels of failure into perpetual motion.

Final Chapter

"Be with a leader when he is right, stay with him when he is still right, but, leave when he is wrong."

Abraham Lincoln

A Solid Foundation

It was Robert E. Lee who said, "the primary responsibility of a leader is to lead properly." His insight, combined with the advice from President Abraham Lincoln, "Be with a leader when he is right, stay with him when he is still right, but, leave when he is wrong," provides us with the road map for moving forward from where many individuals, through no fault of their own, currently find themselves.

Real leaders, the kind worth following, understand the foundation of any successful, dynamic, and vibrant organization is built on a solid foundation. These individuals understand the fundamental building blocks of any dynamic, vibrant, and robust organization are built on trust, integrity, humility, openness, and creativity.

When these five foundational characteristics define the culture of an organization, that organization will grow and prosper because these behaviors naturally attract ethical, well-educated, talented, and mentally well-adapted individuals. When these five values are absent, dysfunction reigns, and the organization crumbles from within; or as Anthony Scaramucci, President Trump's previous White House Director of Communications so eloquently said, "the fish rots from the head."

Each of the thirteen malignant characteristics that comprise the elements found in a Leadership Autopsy Toe Tag work in unison to erode trust, integrity, humility, openness, and creativity. It is essential to understand that a leader cannot model malignant leadership behavior and build a healthy, dynamic, and vibrant organization at the same time. They can either embrace malignant behaviors or reject them, but they cannot do both.

Closing

In 2012, Warren Buffet fired Denis Abrams then CEO of Berkshire Hathaway's Benjamin Moore paint. Abrams served as CEO of Benjamin Moore for a seven-year period starting 2005 – 2012, (How One Executive Rewards Trip Damaged Employee Trust, Jacque Vilet, March 3, 2014, Talent Magazine & HR).

> "Ding! Dong! The witch is dead!" one former exec told The Post, noting that Abrams routinely referred to himself as a "dictator" as he threatened dissenting workers with their jobs (nyposy.com/2012/06/15).

According to *The Post*, "it was because in 2012, Abrams took a group of Benjamin Moore executives on a company-paid yacht trip in Bermuda to celebrate a rise in quarterly sales, the first since 2007 and after the company had suffered through five years of shrinking sales in the wake of the housing market collapse.

The Bermuda trip was said to have upset rank-and-file Benjamin Moore employees, who had been through multiple layoffs, cuts in sales commissions, and frozen salaries over five years of tough times during the Great Recession and its aftermath. No doubt, the "survivors" had to double up on their workload, too. For the record, Warren Buffet has stated that the reason for firing Abrams "was based on a differing view about distribution channels and brand strategy." This statement is consistent with an earlier communication Buffet made in 2000, when Berkshire Hathaway purchased Benjamin Moore. In 2000 Buffet made a promise to existing Benjamin Moore distributors that the business model would not change under his ownership. Denis Abrams was threatening to break that promise, and Buffet fired him.

As the old saying goes, "when one door closes another one opens," and this was certainly the case for Denis Abrams. The newly fired CEO of Benjamin Moore would soon find himself as president and COO of EasyPaint. EasyPaint CEO Marty Cornish welcomed Abrams onboard "as an experienced player with a proven track record of success during his tenure at Benjamin Moore," (technically, December 18, 2015). Marty Cornish could make this statement because he is not a trained Forensic Leadership Pathologist.

Whether Abrams was fired because he failed to understand and execute the vision Warren Buffet had for Benjamin Moore, the result of the toxic organizational culture he had created, or the incredibly poor judgment he showed by celebrating his first success in five years with an all-expense company-paid trip to the Bahamas on a private yacht, with a select group of executives, none of these reasons really matter.

What does matter - in fact, the only thing that matters - is that, according to an insider briefed on the firing of Abrams, as Berkshire Hathaway officials stood by to watch Abrams clear out his office, "Abrams kept asking what he had done wrong," (Business Insider.com June 5, 2012). Denis Abrams was completely unable to grasp the concept that he had done something wrong. He had no idea that he had failed as a leader.

It is essential to recognize that as far as our current collection of leaders go, Denis Abrams is not an outlier; he is the norm. He is the poster boy of typical leadership in business and industry today. Even after being fired by Warren Buffet, and escorted off the premises, Abrams still could not fathom his own complicity in his dismissal. Abrams's failure helps to illustrate the point; you can't fix malignant leaders because malignant leaders do not believe they need fixing, or as a good friend of mine once said, "Pigs don't know pigs stink!" Their dysfunctional behaviors not only got them to their current position, but in many instances, it is only through the continued use of these malignant and dysfunctional behaviors that they will manage to remain in positions of power and authority.

Until recently, the general public has not had access to either the evaluative tools or social media platform necessary to identify and hold malignant leaders personally and publicly accountable for their actions. That partially explains why individuals such as; Thomas Morley, George Ball, Robert Uihlein Jr., Albert Henry Wiggins, Kenneth Winston Starr, Jerry Sandusky, Dr. Graham Spanier, Tim Curley, Gary Schultz, Bernard Ebbers, John Stumpf, Kenneth Lay, Jeffrey Skilling,

Eddie Antar, Elizabeth Holmes, and Ramesh Balwani, were allowed to do what they did.

Because the general public has been led to believe that they lack either the education, experience, or the right titles to comprehend the complexity of leadership, they have come to believe that they are not up to the task of evaluating their leadership. As a result, the next generation of malignant leaders, individuals who have learned at the knees of their predecessors, are queued up and itching for their turn to put the "fun" back in dysfunctional.

Fortunately, as George Orwell would say, "It's a brave new world." As a Forensic Leadership Pathologist, you have the ability, skills, and knowledge to serve as a catalyst to bring about a greater understanding and awareness of malignant leadership practices. You understand what malignant leadership looks like, feels like, and acts like. You are trained in the science of Forensic Leadership Pathology. At this point, you know as much as, or more than, most leaders about malignant leadership. If your leadership looks a train wreck, acts like a train wreck, and sounds like a train wreck, pull out your Toe Tag because you know exactly what to do.

As a trained Forensic Leadership Pathologist, your challenge is two-fold; first, to use your new skills to critically evaluate the impact leadership is having on an organization, and second, to share your findings with the rest of the world. Remember, the goal of a Forensic Leadership Pathologist is not to fix failing leaders. As mentioned earlier, malignant leaders are not interested in being fixed. Your goal is to identify malignant leaders for what they are, so that you, as well as everyone else, can avoid falling victim to them or their dysfunctional behaviors. Choose to be a “Pattern Disrupter” by sharing the results of your Leadership Autopsy Toe Tags with others.

John Stuart Mill said, "The only thing necessary for the triumph of evil is that good men do nothing." As a Forensic Leadership Pathologist, download your Toe Tag and get busy! As a Forensic Leadership Pathologist, you have a scientifically-based method to record and quantify your observations. I encourage you to observe, analyze, and share your findings with any and everyone who will listen to you. Nothing will disrupt the pattern of dysfunction more effectively than informed, intelligent people with voices who know how to use them.

Welcome to the field of Forensic Leadership Pathology. The world needs individuals with the skills, courage, and knowledge to become a disrupter; because one more malignant leader is one to many.

If you have any questions or comments you would like to share, feel free to drop me a line at Fleishmanbooks.com. I look forward to hearing from you.

Leadership Autopsy Toe Tag Forms

Forensic Leadership Analysis TM.			
Evaluator:			
Organization:			
Leadership Autopsy Toe Tag TM			
Instructions: Check "Yes" if behavior is observable. Check "No" if the behavior is not observable. If behavior is present, circle Value. Add all circled scores together to generate a total score. Compare total score to Evaluation Scale.			
Malignant Behaviors	Observed **Yes**	Value	Observed **No**
Lying		6	
Hubris		6	
Avarice		6	
Duplicity		6	
Cunning		5	
Narcissism		5	
Disconnection		5	
Deception		4	
Dismissiveness		4	
Manipulation		4	
Inconsistency		3	
Unteachability		3	
Gamesmanship		3	
	Total Score		
Evaluation Scale	**Levels**		**Action**
Score 40 - 60	Dying Organization		**Run!**
Score 21 - 39	Malignancy Spreading		**Update Resume**
Score 1 - 20	Malignancy Present		**Observe Closely**

Forensic Leadership Analysis TM.			
Evaluator:			
Organization:			
Leadership Autopsy Toe Tag TM			
Instructions: Check "Yes" if behavior is observable. Check "No" if the behavior is not observable. If behavior is present, circle Value. Add all circled scores together to generate a total score. Compare total score to Evaluation Scale.			
Malignant Behaviors	Observed **Yes**	Value	Observed **No**
Lying		6	
Hubris		6	
Avarice		6	
Duplicity		6	
Cunning		5	
Narcissism		5	
Disconnection		5	
Deception		4	
Dismissiveness		4	
Manipulation		4	
Inconsistency		3	
Unteachability		3	
Gamesmanship		3	
	Total Score		
Evaluation Scale	**Levels**		**Action**
Score 40 - 60	Dying Organization		**Run!**
Score 21 - 39	Malignancy Spreading		**Update Resume**
Score 1 - 20	Malignancy Present		**Observe Closely**

Forensic Leadership Analysis TM.			
Evaluator:			
Organization:			
Leadership Autopsy Toe Tag TM			
Instructions: Check "Yes" if behavior is observable. Check "No" if the behavior is not observable. If behavior is present, circle Value. Add all circled scores together to generate a total score. Compare total score to Evaluation Scale.			
Malignant Behaviors	Observed **Yes**	Value	Observed **No**
Lying		6	
Hubris		6	
Avarice		6	
Duplicity		6	
Cunning		5	
Narcissism		5	
Disconnection		5	
Deception		4	
Dismissiveness		4	
Manipulation		4	
Inconsistency		3	
Unteachability		3	
Gamesmanship		3	
	Total Score		
Evaluation Scale	**Levels**		**Action**
Score 40 - 60	Dying Organization		**Run!**
Score 21 - 39	Malignancy Spreading		**Update Resume**
Score 1 - 20	Malignancy Present		**Observe Closely**

Forensic Leadership Analysis ™.			
Evaluator:			
Organization:			
Leadership Autopsy Toe Tag ™			
Instructions: Check "Yes" if behavior is observable. Check "No" if the behavior is not observable. If behavior is present, circle Value. Add all circled scores together to generate a total score. Compare total score to Evaluation Scale.			
Malignant Behaviors	Observed **Yes**	Value	Observed **No**
Lying		6	
Hubris		6	
Avarice		6	
Duplicity		6	
Cunning		5	
Narcissism		5	
Disconnection		5	
Deception		4	
Dismissiveness		4	
Manipulation		4	
Inconsistency		3	
Unteachability		3	
Gamesmanship		3	
	Total Score		
Evaluation Scale	**Levels**		**Action**
Score 40 - 60	Dying Organization		**Run!**
Score 21 - 39	Malignancy Spreading		**Update Resume**
Score 1 - 20	Malignancy Present		**Observe Closely**

Forensic Leadership Analysis TM.			
Evaluator:			
Organization:			
Leadership Autopsy Toe Tag TM			
Instructions: Check "Yes" if behavior is observable. Check "No" if the behavior is not observable. If behavior is present, circle Value. Add all circled scores together to generate a total score. Compare total score to Evaluation Scale.			
Malignant Behaviors	Observed **Yes**	Value	Observed **No**
Lying		6	
Hubris		6	
Avarice		6	
Duplicity		6	
Cunning		5	
Narcissism		5	
Disconnection		5	
Deception		4	
Dismissiveness		4	
Manipulation		4	
Inconsistency		3	
Unteachability		3	
Gamesmanship		3	
	Total Score		
Evaluation Scale	**Levels**		**Action**
Score 40 - 60	Dying Organization		**Run!**
Score 21 - 39	Malignancy Spreading		**Update Resume**
Score 1 - 20	Malignancy Present		**Observe Closely**

Forensic Leadership Analysis TM.

Evaluator:

Organization:

Leadership Autopsy Toe Tag TM

Instructions: Check "Yes" if behavior is observable. Check "No" if the behavior is not observable. If behavior is present, circle Value. Add all circled scores together to generate a total score. Compare total score to Evaluation Scale.

Malignant Behaviors	Observed Yes	Value	Observed No
Lying		6	
Hubris		6	
Avarice		6	
Duplicity		6	
Cunning		5	
Narcissism		5	
Disconnection		5	
Deception		4	
Dismissiveness		4	
Manipulation		4	
Inconsistency		3	
Unteachability		3	
Gamesmanship		3	
	Total Score		

Evaluation Scale	Levels	Action
Score 40 - 60	Dying Organization	**Run!**
Score 21 - 39	Malignancy Spreading	**Update Resume**
Score 1 - 20	Malignancy Present	**Observe Closely**

Forefnsic Leadership Analysis ™.

Forensic Leadership Analysis ™.			
Evaluator:			
Organization:			
Leadership Autopsy Toe Tag ™			
Instructions: Check "Yes" if behavior is observable. Check "No" if the behavior is not observable. If behavior is present, circle Value. Add all circled scores together to generate a total score. Compare total score to Evaluation Scale.			
Malignant Behaviors	Observed **Yes**	Value	Observed **No**
Lying		6	
Hubris		6	
Avarice		6	
Duplicity		6	
Cunning		5	
Narcissism		5	
Disconnection		5	
Deception		4	
Dismissiveness		4	
Manipulation		4	
Inconsistency		3	
Unteachability		3	
Gamesmanship		3	
	Total Score		
Evaluation Scale	**Levels**		**Action**
Score 40 - 60	Dying Organization		**Run!**
Score 21 - 39	Malignancy Spreading		**Update Resume**
Score 1 - 20	Malignancy Present		**Observe Closely**

Made in United States
Cleveland, OH
04 November 2026

47647064R00116